Using 1

Guidance Notes for Investigators
of Apparitions, Hauntings, Poltergeists and Similar Phenomena

STEVEN T. PARSONS

Published in 2021 by Society for Psychical Research
Copyright © Society for Psychical Research

ISBN: 9781916427310
Published by Society for Psychical Research
1 Vernon Mews
London
W14 0RL

Society for Psychical Research

The purpose of the Society for Psychical Research, which was founded in 1882, is to examine without prejudice or prepossession and in a scientific spirit those faculties of man, real or supposed, which appear to be inexplicable on any generally recognised hypothesis. In keeping with most scientific bodies, the Society holds no corporate views. Any opinions expressed in its publications are, therefore, those of the authors alone. For over a century the Society has published an impressive body of evidence for the existence of such faculties and the occurrence of paranormal phenomena.

INTRODUCTION

The overwhelming majority of the evidence relating to cases of haunting and the appearance of ghosts, apparitions and poltergeist phenomena exists in the form of personal testimony and the accounts of witnesses. It is a fact, that to date, no device or item of equipment has yet demonstrated the reality of these, or any similar phenomena.

Some readers might think it is strange to introduce these guidance notes with such a statement. But any discourse relating to the use of equipment for investigating instances of haunting or the manifesting of poltergeists and ghosts, must consider this reality. Does this mean that using equipment for making measurements and gathering data when investigating such cases, is a futile endeavour, driven only by hope, belief and wishful thinking? The answer must be an emphatic no!

The use of equipment has allowed investigators to examine measure and record in the minutest of detail, the environment in places where these phenomena are reported. Careful measurements and observations have been used to test the claims and the reports of witnesses and in many instances the use of equipment has assisted the investigator to determine the cause of an event or reported experience.

Since the beginning of the twentieth century, the use of equipment has become synonymous with the investigation of haunted places. Investigators now have access to an extensive range of devices and gadgets, and they routinely deploy an array of equipment in almost every case they are called upon to examine. Some of these tools may be genuinely helpful, whilst other items owe their existence and use, more to fad and fashion.

To be an effective investigator, the investigator should have a good understanding of the ideas and the theories that both support and contradict the usefulness and purpose of every device and item of equipment that they are using.

These guidance notes are intended to provide helpful information and practical guidance to all those who use equipment to support their investigations. They are also intended to help the investigator to obtain the maximum usefulness from their equipment and from the data they collect whilst using it.

Equipment forms just a part of the investigation of haunted places and anomalous experiences. This publication is intended to be used in conjunction with the general Guidance Notes for Investigators of Spontaneous Cases, published by the society in 2018. This is available separately from the Society for Psychical Research, and includes guidance for interviewing witnesses and gathering information, planning and undertaking an investigation and producing an investigation report.

CONTENTS

1 | The Usefulness of Equipment

As already stated in the introduction, the bulk of the evidence relating to apparitions, hauntings and poltergeists exists only in the form of personal testimony and the accounts of witness's experiences. The investigator should not disregard these accounts, but they must be mindful that these accounts and reports are subjective and they may not always be entirely accurate or reliable. In situations where the investigator seeks to verify or validate a reported experience or an event, their use of equipment may sometimes be helpful, for instance; by making an audio recording of a reported sound or measuring a perceived temperature change.

Equipment can be used to determine the level of a physical variable or the rate by which it is changing. Using equipment can also be used to extend the capabilities of the investigator, especially in situations where it is difficult for the investigator to maintain a long-term presence or to permit the recording of events that occur intermittently or which happen over an extended period of time and may otherwise go unnoticed.

Many investigators consider that the use of equipment is essential. However, a great deal of the investigation process; often the entire investigation, can successfully be carried out without recourse to anything more than a pen and paper.

Investigators may consider that it is advantageous for them to deploy multiple pieces of equipment at every opportunity. Their rationale is to obtain as much information as possible, in the hope of capturing something that might be helpful. This may seem to be a good idea but it also means that the investigator is forced to sift through vast amounts of data or lengthy recordings from the numerous devices. Searching through large amounts of data greatly increases the likelihood that significant details will be missed or overlooked. Using equipment that is unnecessary, can cause disruption for the client too, filling their home or workplace with your equipment, often for little or no return. It is recommended that the investigator limits their use of equipment and deploys items of equipment selectively, being guided by the description of events and the experiences of witnesses. Using equipment in this fashion considerably increases the likelihood of relevant and potentially helpful information being obtained.

1.1 *There will always be exceptions*

An exception to the selective use of equipment for the gathering of data may be those instances when the investigator suspects that the reports indicate it may be a poltergeist case. These often display a wide variety of concurrent activity which may only continue for a short time, sometimes just a few weeks. In these circumstances, the investigator may consider that it is worthwhile for them to deploy multiple items of equipment, in order to gather as much information as is practical in what may be a limited time, for later examination in detail. Video cameras are especially helpful in such instances and it is recommended that the investigator should consider the early use of as many video recording devices as possible.

Although it is unlikely that any investigation would ever be undertaken without at least some notion as to why a particular location is being investigated. Investigators may occasionally encounter a situation where they have very little witness testimony or other information available beforehand. In these circumstances, using equipment in order to gather a range of basic environmental data may prove to be helpful, allowing the investigator to establish and understand the conditions which prevail at the location.

1.2 *Buyer beware*

Devices which claim to be able to detect the presence of ghosts and spirits, or which allow the user to communicate with these supposed entities have been around for over a century. Succeeding iterations of ghost hunting gadgets and apparatus have appeared, each accompanied by a fanfare of hope and promise. Each in turn has been relegated into obscurity when those using them came to realise that they did not deliver upon the claims and promises made about them.

The modern investigator faces a bewildering assortment of devices and software applications (Apps), all of them claiming to assist the investigator in finding the evidence or proof that they are seeking. Some devices gain popularity after an appearance on some ghost hunting show or because of social media hype. Many of these devices and Apps are marketed with impressive claims by their makers and promoters; boasting that their particular device or App will provide the investigator with the capability to detect ghosts or other spirits with unerring reliability or allow the spirits to communicate with astonishing clarity.

Before considering buying and using any of these devices or Apps, the investigator is urged to carefully consider the claims that are being made. They are advised to disregard the glowing reviews, and instead examine the specifications and ask themselves What units of measurement does it use? How are the measurements indicated to the user? How accurate are the measurements? In reality, many of these ghost hunting gadgets arrive with very little information about the way in which they operate. Even fewer present their data using any recognised system of measurement. Many come with adornments that owe more to new age belief than to any recognised scientific theory. Retro steampunk design and the addition of crystals, coloured lights, religious symbols and other esoteric items may add visual appeal but does nothing to improve the quality of the data or usefulness of the information that these devices provide. So far, none of these devices have ever produced any results that have withstood proper scrutiny and critical evaluation. In every case, these gadgets represent a poor investment, financially and in quality of the information they provide to the investigator.

1.3 *Using measurements*

Any measurement data or recording has little value until it has passed a number of stringent tests. It should be examined and considered impartially and without the interference of the investigator's personal beliefs, hopes and desires. A temperature anomaly recorded by a data-logging thermometer is simply an indication that the temperature changed in an unexpected way. Similarly, the existence of an electromagnetic field, even one that appears to have no reasonable explanation is not evidence for the existence of ghosts or spirits.

The role of the investigator is to diligently search for an explanation and to gain an understanding about the experiences of those who have witnessed and reported anomalous phenomena at a particular location. The investigator should always avoid any temptation to rush headlong into proffering an explanation or suggesting a resolution without first obtaining all of the available information pertaining to the case. Only by the appropriate use of the equipment and the application of robust methods for evaluating their recordings and data can the investigator show that they are aware of the numerous potential problems that exist and demonstrate that they have acted to address and mitigate them.

Instead of searching the data for information that may help the investigator to understand the situation, investigators will sometimes scan through the data seeking any irregularities or anomalies. Any inclination by the investigator to focus only on data which they consider to be unusual or which supports an idea or belief should be avoided. Disregarding data which is considered to be less supportive or less important can result in significant information being overlooked. The information that is provided by means of measurement and observation should always be considered in its entirety, regardless of whether it supports or contradicts the accounts of the witness or the ideas and beliefs of the investigator.

The data and measurements that are gathered are just a part of the overall body of evidence and should be used together with all of the other information that is available.

This may come from witness testimony, historical accounts and from previous visits and investigations carried out by others. In some instances, it may become apparent that a particular event takes place with some degree of regularity and patterns may begin to emerge which may indicate a potential cause for the phenomena and experiences. The times at which an event occurred, its duration and the extent or rate of change can often reveal additional detail or indicate when or where further observations and measurements may be required.

Situations in which the investigator is able to objectively record or measure an unusual change that coincides with a reported anomalous experience are potentially of the greatest interest. For example, a witness might report hearing a particular sound at the same time that a temperature change is recorded by the investigator. But coincidental timing alone should not be considered as evidence that either event is connected or that they are anomalous. What the investigator seeks, is objective confirmation of a reported experience and they should always try to determine the cause or source of that event. It may be, that upon further examination, the sound has no relationship with the temperature change. It is also possible that the two events are linked; for example, the sound coming from the operation of a heating or cooling appliance. Examination of the data may suggest other possible causes, each of which the investigator must fully consider and test, perhaps by using additional measurements or by devising further experiments.

2 | Measurement

Measurement is the process of determining the physical properties of an object or an event, for example its magnitude, its rate of change or its duration. Measurements allow the investigator to observe and to record the prevailing conditions and document any changes that may occur within the ambient environment at the investigation site. Measurements can be used to assist the investigator in following the progress of any changes which may take place within the environment and use that information to gain an insight into the processes and causes for any changes that are observed.

2.1 *Units of measurement*

Regardless of whichever variable the investigator intends to measure, it is important that the resulting measurements should always be carried out using one of the accepted measuring systems. For example, with electromagnetic field (EMF) meters it is common to see measurements provided in either units of milliGauss (mG) or MicroTesla (uT). Likewise, the temperature which may be displayed using either degrees Fahrenheit or Celsius.

There are a number of accepted measuring systems in regular use. Science and industry predominantly use the SI (Système International d'Unités) system, which is based upon a metric system of measurement. In the UK, the metric system is now commonplace although there are occasions when imperial measuring units continue in regular use. For example, the use of imperial units for distance (inches, feet and miles), weight (ounces, pounds and stones) and liquid volume (pints and gallons). In the USA, measurements which use the US Customary Units system, which is based upon the British Imperial system of measurement, are still in regular use.

It is recommended that wherever possible the investigator should use the appropriate SI unit of measurement. This may not always be possible, but regardless of whichever measurement system the investigator chooses for a particular variable, they should ensure that all of their measurements of that variable are made using the same units of measurement. Mixing different units of measurement is unhelpful and should be avoided whenever possible in order to minimise confusion or misunderstanding. Many items of equipment will allow the user to select the measurement units they wish to use. The applied measurement setting should be periodically checked, as some devices may default to a different measurement system when they are first switched on, or following a battery change. When it is not possible for the user to select the desired unit of measurement, it may be necessary to apply a conversion factor to the resulting data. If a conversion factor is used, this should be indicated in the investigation notes.

2.2 *Estimating measurements*

In some situations, the only measurements that are available may be estimations. A witness may say that a place feels warmer or colder, or describe a sound becoming louder or quieter. The individual may attempt to quantify the measurement, or offer an analogy to describe their experience; for instance, "the figure was more than six feet high" or "the room became as cold as ice". Whilst this information is helpful and allows the investigator to gain an understanding of the event or the experience, measurements of this type should not be considered as being definitive. Estimated measurements should always be clearly indicated as such in any notes and records.

2.3 *Non-standard measuring systems*

Investigators should avoid using devices and equipment which present their data using a non-standard system of units that does not conform to any of the established measurement systems. For example, a number of commonly used EMF meters only have a series of coloured lights, e.g., red, amber and green, with little, or sometimes no indication how the lights relate to the actual levels of electromagnetism present within a location. Other meters use a scale with indicating lights, each of which covers a range of values, e.g., 1st indicator = 1-3 mG, 2nd indicator = 4-7 mG, 3rd indicator = 7-10 mG etc. Whilst these types of meter may occasionally be useful for obtaining a crude estimation, they should not be used for the purpose of obtaining accurate measurements. Non-standard measurements are difficult, often impossible, to accurately compare against measurements that are made using other devices.

2.4 *Extended measuring over time*

Modern equipment provides the investigator with the capability for making measurements over extended periods of time. Measurements lasting hours, days or in some instance's weeks, are easily achieved. This can be used to provide the investigator with additional information about the location and lets them observe trends such as those which may be caused by human interactions or the weather. This information is invaluable; providing important context and understanding about what is normal for a particular location. Longer term observations and measurements may also reveal patterns that would otherwise have gone unnoticed or may not have been previously considered. In some locations, this may be due to activities and events that are cyclical or which occur only intermittently.

2.5 *Baseline measurements*

Whenever possible, the investigator should seek to make a series of measurements in order to provide a baseline series of data against which the measurements made during the course of the investigation can be compared. Baseline data can be obtained for any of the environmental variables that would normally be measured and observed by the investigator, including audio and video recording.

It is common practise for investigators to make several measurements prior to the commencement of the investigation for the purposes of establishing a baseline. Sometimes, these measurements may have been made under very different conditions from those which exist during the investigation. Baseline measurements should be commenced as soon as possible and continue without interruption throughout the investigation visit. These measurements may easily be undertaken using automated data-logging equipment. It is usually sufficient to use a single measuring device for each of the variables being considered, i.e., a thermometer, EMF meter, audio recorder and camcorder. The placement of this equipment should be such that it best represents the main characteristics of the key areas of interest throughout the location. Manually obtaining baseline data can also be carried out, which although laborious, is nonetheless important and should be done wherever practical. A pre-prepared sheet can be used for this purpose and a separate sheet used for each set of measurements.

2.6 *Preparing to make measurements*

Whenever the investigator intends to make any measurements, it is essential that they are adequately prepared beforehand. Sometimes, an item of measuring equipment may not have been used for some time. It is recommended that each item of equipment is tested to ensure that it is operating correctly. These checks should always be made prior to the investigation, allowing sufficient time to rectify any problems that may be discovered. Occasionally, the investigator may need to use the equipment at short notice. Having a routine of regular checking and testing for each item of equipment saves time and minimises the likelihood of any problems being discovered whilst setting up the equipment.

The investigator should establish a good reason or indication for making every measurement or series of measurements. This might be to verify the experience of a witness or to test a hypothesis relating to some possible cause. Ad hoc measurements, made in the hope of finding something or simply because the equipment has been brought along and it may as well be used, are rarely productive or worthwhile.

The appropriate item of equipment should be selected for each variable that is to be measured. The device or instrument used should be of a suitable quality and should always be used in accordance with the manufacturer's specifications and limitations of use. The measuring precision and accuracy of the device should be known and understood.

The placement of the device or of its sensor should always be optimally located for the variable that is being measured. Due care must be taken to prevent any measurements from being adversely affected by nearby objects and appliances or other measuring devices that are in use. Some devices have multiple sensors and the investigator should ensure that each sensor is used appropriately in order that the measurements that are obtained will be meaningful. Priority should be given to the placing of those sensors intended for measuring variables which are likely to be the most worthwhile i.e., those which may be indicated by witness reports or suggested by other information. This may sometimes mean compromising the position of sensors that are being used to measure lower priority variables. Irrespective of the capabilities of a particular device, there is seldom any value in making measurements of variables that have not been previously indicated and any measurements of these may be disregarded or the sensor switched off.

Measurements should always be carried out using an appropriate measuring technique. For example, when handholding some devices, the proximity of the individual may affect the sensor and make it more difficult to make accurate measurements.

The investigator should recognise that every item of equipment can malfunction and give erroneous readings. Sometimes, this may be due to a damaged sensor or some other failure; most often, this occurs as a result of a weak or flat battery or is due to mishandling. In all instances where an unexpected measurement is discovered, the correct operation of the measuring device should be ascertained. This can be done by comparing it against another similar device or by placing it into a known environment and observing the accuracy of the resulting measurements. It is good practise to assume that all measurements made immediately prior to questionable data should be marked as unreliable and use of the device should be suspended until the investigator has properly tested the devise and if necessary, has rectified any fault that is discovered. If no fault is found when testing the device, the investigator may reasonably assume that the data is correct and work on trying to understand the cause or source of the unexpected measurement.

It is helpful for investigators to have a basic level of knowledge regarding each of the variables which they are measuring. Unfortunately, many investigators continue to use devices without an adequate knowledge of why they are using them or what constitutes a normal series of measurements. This inevitably leads to a misunderstanding that only serves to confuse the investigator and results in wasted effort and contributes to a poor conclusion. It is also common practise during a public access investigation event for items of equipment to be given to individuals with only rudimentary instructions regarding its use. In these instances, it is safer to mark any data which they may obtain as unreliable unless it has been checked and verified at the time by an investigator who is conversant with the proper use of the equipment.

2.7 *Measurements made by others*

Occasionally, the investigator may be provided with data or recordings that were taken by the witness or some other person. These may have been made prior to the involvement of the investigator or they may have been made whilst the investigation is in progress.

An important point regarding any measurements or recordings that are provided by third parties is that the investigator must never disregard the data or the recording merely because it seems too good to be true, or it appears to be unreliable. Nor must it be given too much credibility because it appears to be supportive of one's personal thoughts or ideas. Every item of data should be thoroughly considered and evaluated; the data may sometimes be the only information that is available especially in the early stages of an investigation. It should be tested alongside the supporting testimony or claims that accompany it.

Some locations may have cameras and other monitoring systems already installed. The data from these recording and measuring devices can be a helpful addition to the information that is available to the investigator. The investigator should be wary of accepting any data or recording at face value, however reliable the data collecting system that was used might seem or how truthful the witness might appear. Mistakes and errors do occur, and although fortunately rare, trickery is not unknown.

Each of these additional sources of information should be evaluated in exactly the same manner as the data and recordings that are made by the investigator. However, any data which has been collected by a person or system that is independent of the investigator and outside of their control must be given an additional degree of scrutiny. The first thing to check is the date and time of the recording or measurement; if this does not appear to agree with the testimony or account of the witness then its value becomes significantly weakened. Of course, it is highly likely that the person or someone in charge of the equipment may simply have forgotten to set the date and time; there are countless examples of this on security camera footage shown on television every week. The investigator should check that the data or recording they have been given is actually the correct item. It is not unknown for the wrong set of environmental data to be sent. If the information has been verified as being correct but the date / time is incorrect, then the investigator should acknowledge the problem and should not try to disguise or hide it in any way. Neither should they present it without comment. It is important that the investigator can demonstrate that they are aware of the problem and show that they have acted to deal with it.

The investigator should also attempt to ascertain the type of equipment or device that was used to make the measurements or recordings and check that this agrees with the type of file that has been provided. For example, if the witness says that a particular video was taken using an iPhone, the investigator should determine precisely which model of iPhone was used. The camera systems and the way in which the image data is processed changes from generation to generation of the phone, and in some instances, this can provide the investigator with a better understanding about how the image may have been produced.

Some equipment manufacturers use a distinctive prefix for their image or data files or use a particular format for storing or exporting the information. Others may append a digital signature or use some other means for making their data identifiable; this is often done to protect the intellectual copyright of the maker but it can also be helpful for the investigator.

3 | Documenting and Recording Measurements

Making accurate measurements is only a part of the information and data gathering process and the importance of accurately recording the various measurements must not be overlooked. The investigator will often use a variety of devices and take a great many measurements during the course of each investigation. It is therefore essential that the investigator develops a reliable and robust method for recording every item of information. This will ensure that the data can be correctly interpreted and used in order to produce an accurate record of the investigation and to support their findings or conclusions.

An increasing number of the devices that are used by investigators are capable of automated measuring and recording; saving the information as a small software file which can be examined at a convenient time. Memory cards used for holding the stored data should be labelled, indicating when and where the data was obtained. This can be in the form of a note which clearly indicates the card's use and the item of equipment it was used with. There are many devices, which still require their measurements to be made and recorded manually. In these circumstances, using a pre-prepared sheet or chart for each device, with suitable spaces that can be filled in as required during the investigation is recommended.

Whichever method for recording measurements is used, the investigator should ensure that the information which has been gathered can be easily understood and correctly interpreted at a later date. The use of abbreviations, codes and jargon should be avoided and the same method for recording information should be used by all participants. Investigation teams should ensure that every team member receives adequate instructions regarding the importance of accurately documenting any measurements they may make. Oftentimes, individuals may be using their personal items of equipment and it is important that they are using the same system of measuring as other team members. Using multiple systems of measurement for recording the same variable risks confusion and misunderstanding.

Good record keeping extends beyond just noting down a series of measurements. Without context, measurements are merely numbers that have little value to the investigator. It is important to know where each measurement was obtained, which device was used and most importantly when each measurement was made. Every measurement should be individually time-indexed. For devices that have automated recording, this means ensuring that the device's internal clock is correctly set. With measurements that need to be recorded manually, care must be taken to ensure that every measurement is accurately time-referenced using a watch or clock that has been correctly adjusted with respect to the designated master clock.

It is common practise for investigators to walk around a location, making multiple measurements and trusting either to memory or to a scrap of paper the locations and the times where a device was used and measurements were made. This technique can result in significant errors. Locations can be misremembered; the scrap of paper can be lost or measurements disregarded because the person didn't consider that they were significant or worthwhile either at the time or afterwards.

The investigator should ensure that the location of every measurement or recording is known. The placement of the individual device or sensor must also be documented in a way that allows the location to be easily identified afterwards. This information allows the investigator to correctly link the measurements to both the measuring device that was used and its location at the time the measurements were made. This is particularly important for devices which may be used in several different locations during the investigation. Whenever a device is moved to a different location, the new position should be recorded together with the time that this was done. It is important to include sufficient information to allow the exact location in which the measurements were taken to be easily identified. For example, writing "On the stairs", provides very little useful information about the device's whereabouts on the stairs or even, in some locations, which staircase the note refers to. Whereas a little more information, e.g., "Stairs, 3 treads up from ground floor, in centre of stair tread" or "Rear corridor stairs, 4 treads down from top, attached to vertical handrail, 1-foot above tread height" is much more helpful to understanding a device's position at a later date.

Unless the location already has a pre-existing system for naming or designating individual rooms and areas, it may be helpful for the investigator to implement a system that identifies each of the investigation areas. This should be done before the investigation commences and used by all of the participants throughout the entire investigation. However, investigators should avoid using names that are suggestive or presumptive; for example, 'The Haunted Bedroom' or 'The Cold Corridor'.

In any instance where part of the measurement record is incomplete or if measurements are discovered to be missing or illegible, the affected portion of the records should be left blank and the missing information clearly acknowledged. Falsifying or attempting to fill gaps in the data afterwards, for whatever reason, will render the entire investigation as being unreliable and may result in the integrity of the investigator or their conclusions being seriously questioned.

3.1 *Using data responsibly*

Investigators who use equipment to support their investigations must ensure that the data they gather is used responsibly. Some of the equipment can be intrusive and whilst it is helpful to know precisely when and where a picture was taken, it may adversely compromise the privacy of the witness or of a location.

A great deal of the equipment used is now connected to the internet and this makes it easy to upload data during the investigation, for later examination. This data may also contain location information which the investigator may not always be aware of. Some Apps may routinely track the location of the device that is being used and there are instances of unauthorised access to the device itself, accessing the camera and microphone without the user being aware. Data stored in cloud servers can also be hacked and the content accessed by unauthorised individuals.

Obviously, the majority of the data and information that is routinely collected by investigators will rarely contain material that is highly sensitive but notes and investigation reports sometimes contain information about a person's mental and physical health, medications and domestic circumstances. The witness is often compliant and may give details willingly or allow access to personal information with few restrictions. It is incumbent upon the investigator to ensure that they do everything possible to safeguard the client and handle every item of data and information in a responsible manner. They should also ensure that the information which is collected and the manner with which it is handled, complies with the relevant requirements of data protection legislation.

3.2 *Producing a report*

The final step of any investigation is usually to produce a report that brings together all of the information and the steps that have been carried out, together with the findings and any conclusions that have been reached. In some instances, the report may only be for the client and the investigator's records. Sometimes, the report may be intended to be shared publicly, or privately with other individuals or organisations. When compiling their report, investigators should assiduously avoid speculation or citing untestable theories, however personally compelling they may be.

Where it is necessary to include data within the report this should be done in such a way that it is clear and understandable. Adding pages of measurements or endless numbers is unlikely to be appreciated and is equally unlikely to help the reader. Data that is included within the report should be relevant; either to support a conclusion or to illustrate a process or condition. In some instances, it may be necessary to include more extensive data; this may often be better placed into an appendix, with only key points included within the main body of the report.

Data should be clearly labelled and if it is decided to present any data in graphical form, this should be done without colour coding different sets of data; many people use a monochrome printer which may not properly show the data. It is also helpful to include some information about the devices that were used for making any measurements and recordings, together with the rationale and reasons for making them. This too, may be included in an appendix to the main body of the report.

The need to protect the privacy of the client is paramount. Data should be carefully checked to ensure that any geo-tags or other identifying information has been completely removed. This is of particular importance with any photographs and videos that are included within the report. However, when producing a report intended only for the client or the records of the investigator, it is usually acceptable to include all of the details pertaining to the location. In all other circumstances, personal information must either be anonymised or removed from within the report.

3.3 *Archiving the data*

Investigations often generate a lot of data, which may need to be retained after the investigation is complete. The data is likely to be in a number of formats including image files, audio recordings and hand written measurement sheets.

It is suggested that all of the data is retained for a period of time following the investigation; occasionally, it may be necessary to re-evaluate or review some of the data, or in some instances the investigator may need to recommence investigating the case. Electronic data should always be stored away from heat and strong magnetic fields. Memory cards and other removeable media should be individually labelled clearly indicating to which case the media and the data or recordings it contains belongs. Avoid using compact discs for storing pictures and video recordings, as over time, the disc may physically deteriorate and become unreadable.

If the information is in the form of an analogue or other tape recording e.g., audio cassette, Hi8 or Digital 8, make a single digital copy at the highest quality settings that are available. Audio and especially video and picture formats do periodically change so it is better to use a standard format such as QuickTime's .mov or .jpg, as these will be less likely to become incompatible with future software. If future formats do change, then it may be necessary to re-copy the images or videos using the newer format. After copying., the original cassette or memory card, should be placed in a dry, cool pace, well away from any magnets or electrical appliances.

After a sufficient time has elapsed, it may be worthwhile sifting through the records in order to determine which information is worth retaining as part of the investigator's archive. This may be more easily facilitated by transferring paper records into an electronic format, either by scanning or photographing. Archival storage should ideally be duplicated, and to prevent potential loss of the archive in the future, cloud-only storage options should be considered in circumstances where local storage is restricted. Cloud storage options may be helpful in circumstances where the investigator wishes to store data that is of a lesser importance but when there may be some potential value in retaining it.

4 | Care and Maintenance

It is not unusual for an investigator or team to have acquired many hundreds or even thousands of pounds worth of equipment. It is therefore of some importance that this equipment is properly protected and cared for. Not only because it represents a significant financial commitment, but more importantly, because the usefulness and value of every observation and measurement made using the equipment requires that it performs reliably and to its specified capabilities. Electronic devices need regular care and also regular use in order to maintain their proper function and reliability. It is not enough to take a device out of a box or bag, turn it on and expect it to perform flawlessly, trusting the measurements to be accurate and reliable. We are familiar with cars requiring regular servicing and routine checks to ensure their continued and reliable operation and a similar degree of attention should also be given to the various items of equipment that the investigator will have amassed.

4.1 *Storage and transport*

Investigation equipment is likely to be used in a variety of locations and situations and this means moving it from place to place and storing it in-between times. Modern electronic equipment is normally robust but it can be easily damaged by improper storage and transportation. Proper consideration should be given to the way each item of equipment is stored and transported and there are many suitable options that are available. Flight cases, either metal or plastic are a popular choice, most have a customisable interior that can be adapted to accommodate several items. Camera bags are also popular and have numerous pockets and compartments into which items can be placed. Occasionally, an item of equipment is supplied with a purpose made case or bag, designed by manufacturer to protect the individual piece of equipment. All of the foregoing provides a good level of physical protection for the equipment.

Using or storing equipment in cold or damp environments can cause problems with condensation forming inside the device which can damage delicate electronic components. When it is not being used, equipment should always be stored in dry conditions, avoiding extremes of temperature and humidity. Garages, outbuildings and attics may not be the best locations for storing equipment unless they are properly insulated and dry. Leaving equipment in a vehicle for long periods is also not recommended as the temperature inside can vary widely between extremes of heat and cold.

Condensation often occurs whenever a device is taken from a cold location into a warmer environment. Condensation can cause a device to malfunction and batteries to drain unexpectedly. It is also a frequency cause for some of the anomalies that are observed in photographs and seen on videos.

These problems can be minimised by placing moisture absorbing silica gel packs in each equipment bag or case and allowing sufficient time for the device to acclimatise to the new temperature before it is switched on and used.

4.2 *Handle with care*

Manufacturers normally provide some basic information about the care and maintenance of equipment in the instruction manual. This usually takes the form of warnings not to drop the device, avoid extremes of temperature, keep it away from water and remove the batteries when not in use. This is important advice and should be followed. However, during many investigations it is common to see items of equipment being passed between individuals with little regard to careful or proper handling. Some investigators also offer or allow members of the public an opportunity to use items of equipment. Sometimes, they may be given only rudimentary instructions regarding the way in which the equipment should be operated, handled and cared for. Equipment is regularly seen left on tables in close proximity to food and drink, shoved into a pocket or put down on the floor, to be trodden upon or accidently kicked. Sometimes, the damage caused by mishandling may not be apparent but can result in the device malfunctioning and giving false readings that may mislead the investigator.

After every investigation, each device should be checked to ensure that it is working correctly before being carefully packed away. Whenever a device is unlikely to be used again for some time, it is recommended that the batteries be removed and stored separately. During extended periods of storage, equipment should be periodically switched on and operated in order to check that the device is operating correctly and to detect any storage problems. It is not unknown for devices to have been put away whilst they are still switched on; if left unattended and unnoticed, the depleted batteries can begin to leak and corrode inside the equipment, permanently damaging it. Prior to use, each device should be re-checked and re-tested to ensure it is working correctly.

A frequent cause of picture anomalies is dirt, or damage to the lens. A dirty or damaged lens can cause a loss of definition or cause an unexpected anomaly to be present in the picture. The lens should always be inspected before use, and if necessary, cleaned using an appropriate cleaning cloth and lens cleaning solution. Avoid any attempt at cleaning the lens using the cuff of a sleeve or some other handy item of clothing. Whenever possible a lens cover should be used to provide physical protection for the lens. Camera-phones often have the front of the lens permanently exposed, greatly increasing the likelihood of it becoming contaminated by dirt and finger prints or being permanently scratched and damaged by items in the user's pocket or bag. Many people place their phone down on any convenient surface with little regard to the exposed camera lens. The investigator should pay particular attention to the lens if they are intending to use their camera-phone during an investigation, ensuring that it is clean and undamaged.

Cameras which have a removeable lens, for example digital single lens reflex (DSLR) models, are susceptible to dirt or dust falling onto the sensor whenever the lens is removed or changed. This causes dark spots to appear in the image, and over time these can increase in number. Some cameras have a sensor cleaning mode which should be used periodically and in extreme cases the user may wish to use one of the dedicated sensor cleaning kits that are available.

4.3 *Battery care*

The importance of batteries and of good battery care is often overlooked by investigators. There are many accounts of batteries that unexpectedly lose their charge, rendering the investigator's equipment useless. Sometimes, the charge is restored and the equipment begins to work once more. Both are commonly attributed to having a paranormal cause. In reality, the majority of these occurrences are the result of inadequate battery care, incorrect understanding of battery performance or simply a poor choice of battery type.

It is important to understand that there are several different types of battery technology which are available, e.g., Lithium, metal-hydride and alkaline and not all of them will have the same performance. For example, metal-hydride and alkaline batteries deliver significantly less power when they are used in colder environments and this can lead to sudden low battery warnings or devices unexpectedly shutting down. When the battery subsequently warms up, either by moving equipment to a warmer location or by holding the battery in the hands for a few minutes, normal power delivery and functioning of the device is often restored.

Different types of battery technology also require different methods in order to maintain reliable operation. Lithium and metal-hydride batteries can be recharged many times but each type of battery requires different methods for charging and storage. For example, battery makers recommend Lithium batteries should be stored with around 50% - 80% of full charge, whilst metal-hydride batteries should be fully charged prior to storage. In both instances, the battery should only be fully charged to 100% immediately before use. The battery manufacturer's advice about their various products should be consulted regarding specific care and use information and the type of charger which should be used to maximise battery life and minimise battery failures. With Lithium batteries in particular, the wrong type of charger can cause the battery to explode or to catch fire.

Batteries do not last forever and over time they will deteriorate. Rechargeable batteries will hold less charge as they age and as they are used. A typical rechargeable battery may be charged and discharged between 500 and 1000 times before it should be replaced. Batteries that are several years old, irrespective of the number of charging cycles they have undergone, will inevitably deteriorate and should be replaced every three to five years. Non-rechargeable batteries will normally have a best before date stamped onto the packaging or the battery. The closer they are to this date, the more likely it will be that their performance will have deteriorated; in most instances, they will still work after this date but their performance will be unreliable.

One of the biggest causes of battery related problems is simply poor battery choice. All batteries, however similar they may appear, are not the same and it is not uncommon to see devices costing hundreds of pounds being used with bargain store batteries. It is recommended to always use good quality batteries and avoid using low-cost unbranded batteries whenever possible. These may be cheaper, but they are also more likely to suffer from poor power delivery, shortened life and leakage, allowing the corrosive chemicals inside the battery to damage equipment.

Carrying batteries loose inside bags and pockets should always be avoided. This can cause individual batteries to become discharged if they come into contact with one another or with other items that are electrically conductive. This is particularly important with Lithium batteries, which can overheat and catch fire if they are accidently discharged in this way. Batteries should be carried so that their terminals are fully insulated from one another and their surroundings.

Many items of equipment require several batteries to be fitted. To ensure the most reliable operation of the device, batteries should be of the same make and type and they should all be changed or charged at the same time. Users should never mix non-rechargeable and rechargeable batteries in the same device as they have different operating voltages and doing so will cause serious damage to the equipment.

4.4 *Memory cards and storage media*

A number of the devices that are used during an investigation require additional, replaceable items in order for them to function properly. Items including tapes, discs or memory cards are often given little thought by the investigator but they can be easily damaged by poor storage and handling or lost altogether. It is also possible for a card that was previously used to be accidentally put into another item of equipment which may erase the data that was previously gathered or may cause the equipment to malfunction. Memory cards should be labelled, indicating which item of equipment they are intended to be used with and stored in the plastic case that is often supplied with the card or in a card case which can be inexpensively obtained. It is also a good idea to have separate storage for cards which have been used and contain investigation data.

The maximum speed of data transfer from and to a memory card is normally marked on the card together with a code indicating the card's speed class. This is the ability of the card to sustain high speed data transfer rates. There are wide discrepancies in the speed at which memory cards of the same type, e.g., SD or microSD are able to store large amounts of data. Using an incorrectly speed rated card can result in data buffering and other problems. This is most likely to happen with video cameras and audio recorders, several of which require a specific class of memory card in order to work correctly. For example, several 4K camcorders must be used with a specific class of memory card in order for them to use their highest video resolutions and some audio recorders will restrict the sampling rate unless a high-speed class card is used. To ensure the optimal performance from any device, the investigator should always use the type and class of memory card that is specified by the manufacturer.

Cheap memory cards may appear to be almost identical to those which are specified and some may appear to work. Sometimes these cards are seconds, offered by the manufacturer for use in less demanding devices or they may be one of the many counterfeit items that are regularly offered for sale. Using a counterfeit memory card can result in the device malfunctioning or even failing completely. It is usually possible to restore normal operation by using a card of the correct specification but it is not unknown for permanent damage to be caused from using a counterfeit memory card.

External hard drives are typically less robust than memory cards. Some of these external hard disks use a rotating storage platter which is easily damaged and the contents lost. They are also susceptible to condensation and to water or moisture. Solid state storage devices are generally more robust but these should still be treated with care. External hard drives normally require some form of cable, e.g., a USB cable, to connect them with the device. Problems caused by using an incorrect cable are not uncommon, even if the cable has the correct connector and fits the drive. For example, some USB cables are designed to only supply power to a device and cannot be used for data.

A number of investigators still use audio cassette recorders or video cameras which use a magnetic tape to store the recording. Video and audio cassettes can easily be damaged by careless handling and poor storage. When not in use, they should be kept in the supplied case and labelled after use. Some of the recent ghost hunting devices that are used by investigators contain very strong neodymium magnets. These can easily erase or damage the information on any video or audio cassette that is placed in close proximity to one of these devices. The powerful magnets may also cause problems with some external hard drives which have a spinning magnetic platter.

4.5 *Accessories*

In addition to the devices themselves, investigators are likely to also use a considerable number of accessories including cables, tripods, microphones and external sensors. These ancillary items should not be neglected. Cables and power cords should be wiped clean of any dirt or moisture and neatly stored after use in order to avoid kinks and prevent breakages from occurring. Cables and wires should be regularly inspected for damage to the insulation and exposed wiring. Plugs and connectors, both on the accessory and the device itself, should be inspected for damage and for dirt and debris that may prevent a proper connection from being made. Bent or misaligned connecting pins are a common cause of problems which can sometimes be easily rectified by gently re-aligning the pin. It may be helpful to label connectors and indicate their correct fitting alignment with a marker pen.

Cable drums or reels are a worthwhile investment; using them reduces the likelihood of damage and can save time when setting up and packing away during the investigation. These can often be acquired for little or no cost from a local electrical retailer or high street stores which sell lengths of cable and wire; some investigators use garden hosepipe reels for storing larger lengths of cable. It is a good idea to label any cables and power cords with their length and their intended purpose or device.

A malfunctioning accessory can easily result in misleading measurements and it may not always be immediately apparent when an accessory is faulty. Many accessories contain batteries or delicate components which can be easily damaged by poor maintenance, careless handling or as a result of poor storage and transport. In the same manner as other items of equipment, the investigator should take care to ensure that all of their accessories are adequately protected and condensation is avoided.

Tripods and microphone stands are commonly used accessories. In addition to holding cameras and microphones, they are also useful for supporting various sensors. It is often necessary for several to be deployed around an investigation site, often in areas where there are numbers of people moving around. Making tripods and stands as conspicuous as possible reduces the risk of them becoming a trip hazard or being knocked over, damaging the equipment they are holding. Strips of brightly coloured reflective or luminous (glow in the dark) tape can be applied to make them more visible. Some may prefer to paint their tripods and stands white or some other light colour. In situations where it is necessary for them to be used in darkness or in very low light levels, attaching one or two chemical glow-sticks to the tripod or stand using adhesive tape or elastic bands is suggested.

Accessories should always be thoroughly checked prior to each investigation to ensure that they are working correctly and visually inspected before packing them away to ensure that any damage which may have occurred can be identified and if necessary, repaired or replaced in good time for the next investigation.

5 | Date and Time

Investigators frequently overlook the importance of accurately recording the time and sometimes even the date, when recording their observations and measurements. Failing to accurately record the time and date not only severely hampers the investigator's ability to take full advantage of the information they have collected; it also substantially undermines the integrity of the entire investigation and the credibility of their results.

Accurately knowing the time when an event occurred or a measurement was made is important when the investigator is attempting to understand the sequence of events and the context of their measurements. For example, there may be instances during an investigation where one or more individuals report experiencing some type of phenomena, seemingly at the same time. Sometimes these reports may come from different parts of the location and without accurate time information for each individual report, it is extremely difficult for the investigator to establish a sequence for the reported events or to determine if there is any relationship between them.

Alternatively, the investigator may wish to check recordings or measurements that were being made at the time a reported experience took place. Without accurate time keeping, this becomes a much more difficult proposition, hampering their ability to precisely establish when measurements were carried out, over what duration they were made and how frequently they were updated. As a result, it becomes much harder to determine if any relationship exists between the reported experiences and information obtained from the equipment.

When presenting their findings or their conclusions, either to the client or for peer review, it is important that the investigator is able to demonstrate that they have properly recorded the time of each event, report or measurement. It is not uncommon to see investigation reports that include photographs showing an incorrect date, sometimes from several years preceding the actual investigation date. This is invariably because someone forgot to set the date and time on the camera. Occasionally, mistakes will happen and they should always be acknowledged and explained in the report.

5.1 *Witness reports and diaries*

It is difficult for the investigator to ensure that the recording of time and date information is accurately maintained in any witness diaries that are being kept. They should stress upon those keeping a diary the importance of recording the date and the time for each entry but the investigator cannot ever be certain that the information will be entirely accurate. It may also be helpful to supply the witness with a notebook or folder for the purposes of diary keeping with a brief note, on the cover, reminding anyone filling in the diary to include the date and time information for each entry.

5.2 *Synchronising the time*

To ensure the accuracy of time keeping and time stamping the measurements, observations and reports made during an investigation, it is necessary to synchronise not only the personal time-keeping device of each individual who is present but also the built-in clock in every applicable item of equipment. Synchronising the time should be done before the commencement of the investigation, normally upon arrival at the location. To avoid this important step from becoming overlooked it is suggested that the group appoint a member to oversee this task.

5.3 *Use a master clock*

A simple method of synchronising the various devices is by the use of a master clock.

Prior to commencing every investigation visit, a master clock should be selected and used as the timing reference by every participant and for setting the time on each of the devices. The master clock can be almost any time-keeping device including a wristwatch, desktop clock, computer or a smart phone. The chosen master clock is not required to have great accuracy with respect to the actual time but it should be capable of keeping good time. Whichever master-clock is decided upon, it is important that it should remain in use as the master-clock for the entirety of that particular investigation visit.

After the master clock has been chosen, each of the time-keeping devices used by individual members of the team should be synchronised with the designated master clock. Every device which has a built-in clock, including personally owned devices, should also be synchronised with the master clock. The importance of this step should not be overlooked or any presumption made that the built-in clock in some devices is already sufficiently accurate and does not need to be checked. It is common for investigators to use a mobile phone or similar network connected device which is able to automatically set itself to the correct time using the network connection. Normally, these are highly accurate, sometimes to fractions of a second, but it is not unknown for them to become set to the wrong time-zone or to suffer from some other loss of synchronicity. Therefore, prior to the commencement of every investigation visit every member of the investigation team should check the accuracy and synchronicity of their personal time-keeping device against the master clock.

5.4 *Synchronise the equipment time*

Many of the devices and items of equipment which are commonly used during an investigation have the capability to record the date and time. Almost every camera, video camera or audio recorder has a built-in clock, allowing it record the time and date whenever a picture is taken or a recording is made. Devices which record measurements either continuously or periodically, e.g., data-logging devices, also require an internal clock in order to accurately time reference the measurements as they are made. The accuracy of these built-in clocks frequently relies upon the user setting the time and date information prior to use. Sometimes, the user will be required to do this manually and some slight variation in the time setting on different items of equipment becomes inevitable.

Wherever possible, the investigator should aim to synchronise all of their devices to an accuracy of within plus or minus five seconds of the master clock time. The actual method for setting the time will vary by device and is normally found within the instructions or user manual. Investigators should always check and never just presume that items of equipment which set the time and date automatically have done so correctly. It is not uncommon for a device to select the wrong time zone, fail to allow for seasonal time adjustments or to simply malfunction. Some devices may require the time and date to be periodically re-set, such as after a battery change or a data reset.

6 | Temperature

Descriptions of sudden and unexpected changes in the ambient temperature are common in cases of haunted houses and other locations. Many of these are likely to have come about due to mismeasuring, or misperception caused by a variety of physiological and psychological factors. Nevertheless, investigators should always consider the importance of measuring the temperature whenever it is indicated by witness accounts.

In addition to the wealth of anecdotal evidence, there are a small number of instances where an unusual temperature change has been recorded by investigators who were using accurate measuring equipment and good measurement methods. Temperature is perhaps one of the most interesting physical variables that an investigator may observe and measure.

6.1 *Choosing a thermometer*

There are a variety of thermometer designs and methods by which the temperature may be measured. From basic liquid in a glass tube models, to devices that have a precision sensor and automated data-logging. Thermometers may be considered as being in two main categories; those which must be placed into direct contact with the object or medium they are measuring and those which require no direct contact with what is being measured.

The accuracy of a thermometer depends upon its design and the manner in which it is used. It is unlikely that many investigators will ever require a highly responsive, milli-degree accurate scientific model, which is also an expensive option. Inexpensive devices may be slightly less accurate or they may respond more slowly to changing temperature, but they are perfectly adequate for the type of temperature measurements that are ordinarily required by investigators. Thermometer manufacturers will normally state the accuracy of their device in the instruction sheet or within its specifications; users are advised to avoid any device where this information is not supplied.

The ambient air temperature at an investigation site is unlikely to ever be excessive and any temperature changes are likely to be in the order of just a few degrees. Therefore, selecting a thermometer with an operating range that extends from a few degrees below the freezing point of water (0°C / 32°F) to a few degrees above the boiling point of water (100°C / 212°F), will normally suffice for the majority, if not all, investigation temperature measurements.

An important consideration when choosing a thermometer is its sampling or refresh rate. This only applies to electronic thermometers which sample the temperature and then update their display periodically. Sampling of the temperature may take place several times every second in scientific or industrial models, or much less frequently; perhaps only once every few minutes for thermometers that are intended for domestic use. The sampling rate does not affect the overall accuracy but models with a long interval between samples may limit the investigator's ability to discern more rapid temperature changes.

The selected thermometer should always be appropriate for the intended use. Using a thermometer that is designed for taking the temperature inside an oven whilst cooking food, or for use in a fish tank or vivarium is more likely to result in inaccurate measurements and the investigation methods being questioned.

6.2 *Direct contact thermometers*

For measuring the ambient temperature and for other general uses, a thermometer which requires its sensor to be placed into direct contact with the material that is being measured (including air) is recommended. Modern thermometers often appear similar, with the sensor either mounted internally or connected to the display with a wire. Different sensor designs are available for measuring the temperature in this way but a thermocouple sensor is perhaps the most useful.

A thermocouple ordinarily consists of a pair of thin sturdy wires, joined together with their junction left bare and exposed to create the sensor. The exposed sensor rapidly responds to any temperature change and when there is a requirement for measuring the temperature of a solid surface, the sensor can easily be attached to the surface with adhesive tape. Thermocouples are robust and have a high degree of accuracy and precision. Thermocouples are available in a number of types and measuring ranges. These are differentiated by a designation letter; for investigation use, a type-K thermocouple will normally be the most suitable. Thermometers using this type of sensor predominantly have a digital display and an ability to present the data in various ways or record it over a period of time. Some thermometers allow the thermocouple to be easily unplugged and replaced; replacements can be acquired for just a few pounds. They are available in various lengths, allowing both the sensor and the thermometer to be conveniently positioned.

The other type of sensor that is commonly used has an electronic component, e.g., a resistor, that varies its electrical characteristics in response to temperature changes. These sensors may be mounted inside the thermometer or attached by a length of wire. The external sensor is similar in appearance to a thermocouple, but they can usually be easily distinguished by having some form of plastic or metal cover at the end of the wire to protect the delicate sensor. The need for physical protection can reduce their speed of response to changes in the surrounding temperature, but in most situations, this is not usually a significant problem nor a reason to avoid using this type of sensor. The protected sensor is often water resistant, making it suitable for immersing into liquids, and for use measuring the temperature of a solid surface, the sensor can be placed upon the surface and secured in the same way as a thermocouple. Some thermometers, that are specifically intended for measuring air temperature, may use an exposed electronic sensor; this responds more quickly to any temperature change, but it can be easily damaged. Temperature information is normally displayed digitally and options for showing additional information and data-logging the measurements are available. Sensors are rarely replaceable if they become damaged and the user is confined to the fixed length of wire that is supplied.

There are also several other types of thermometer that directly measure the temperature of their surroundings. These include models that use a liquid in a glass tube or the expansion and contraction of a metal spring in order to indicate the temperature. These simple designs may be helpful in some circumstances, when only a general indication of the temperature is required, but they are often slow to respond to changing temperature and the analogue scale or dial that they have can be difficult to accurately read.

With all types of direct contact thermometer, it is important to ensure that the sensor is given sufficient time to properly respond to the temperature of its surroundings or the object to which it is attached. This may be anything from a few seconds with some thermocouples to several minutes with a thermometer that uses an internal sensor or a covered sensor. By observing the display, the investigator can judge when to make the measurement.

6.3 *Non-contact thermometers*

In some instances, it may not be possible for the investigator to place the thermometer's sensor into direct contact with the object that they wish to measure. Fortunately, it is possible to remotely measure the temperature of an object by using a thermometer which can determine the temperature based upon the amount of infra-red (thermal) radiation that it emits.

Infra-red thermometers are a popular choice for investigators and can be used for making many types of temperature measurement. They are easy to use, needing only to be pointed towards the object or surface. Many, incorporate a laser spot or ring to assist the user when aiming the device and this often results in them being referred to as 'laser' thermometers. The infra-red temperature sensor used is capable of reacting quickly to changes in temperature and this type of thermometer is typically used for taking an instantaneous measurement of an object's temperature. A significant drawback with this method of measuring temperature is that it is incapable of measuring the temperature of a gas. Investigators attempting to use this type of thermometer for measuring the air temperature will in fact be measuring the temperature of any object or surface which is in view of the sensor, such as a wall, floor or person.

Infra-red thermometers require some form of lens to be used for focussing the IR radiation onto the sensor. Like an optical lens this results in the device having a field of view which increases in area as the distance from the thermometer is increased. This can be likened to an invisible cone extending in front of the sensor. To ensure accuracy, the object being measured should always completely fill or exceed the sensor's field of view. If the thermometer is located too far from the object being measured, unwanted regions surrounding the object will be included and an erroneous measurement will be displayed. The field of view is normally indicated on the body of the thermometer as the distance to spot ratio (D/S Ratio). Some models have the D/S ratio marked on the device in the form of a diagram, indicating the distance from the thermometer and the size of measuring area. Other models may simply state the D/S ratio, either in the manual or marked upon the body of the thermometer. As an example, a D/S ratio of 8:1 indicates that the thermometer will measure the temperature of everything within a 1-inch diameter circular area from a distance of 8 inches from the sensor; the measured area increases to a 3-inch diameter circle at 24 inches distance. Contrary to the way in which infra-red thermometers are often used, reliable measurements are rarely obtainable at distances exceeding four to six feet from the sensor. Aiming it across a large room or space will almost always result in a measurement that is highly inaccurate.

There are numerous different infra-red thermometers available, some costing just a few pounds. These inexpensive devices may seem an attractive choice and, in some instances, they will adequately serve the needs of the investigator. However, these models may use components which are less robust or their measurements may be less reliable. Several models are available which are not intended or suitable for accurately measuring human skin temperature; this may not always be indicated by the seller or on the packaging, and it is important that investigators who desire to use a thermometer in this way should check its specifications carefully. All models present their data digitally and several include an ability to record the data to an internal memory.

6.4 *Emissivity*

An important consideration when using any infra-red thermometer is that different materials and surface finishes have different abilities to emit infra-red energy, even when they are at the same temperature. The ability of an object or surface to emit infra-red radiation is indicated by referring to its emissivity value or factor. This can range from a value of 0.0 (Zero) for a perfect silver mirror, up to a value of 1.0 for a perfect thermal emitter, also called a thermal blackbody, as these have deep matt black appearance. Some common emissivity values include human skin which has an emissivity value of somewhere around 0.95 to 0.98, whilst fabrics, wood and painted surfaces generally have an emissivity of between 0.6 and 0.97.

The majority of infra-red thermometers will have their emissivity pre-set by the manufacturer to a value in the region of 0.95. This value allows the user to make a reasonable assessment of the temperature for most applications, within a margin of error caused by variations in the emissivity value of different surfaces and materials. Some models allow the user to change the emissivity value in order to permit more accurate temperature measurements to be made. In the majority of investigation situations, using an emissivity value of 0.95 will provide measurements that are accurate to within a few degrees of the true temperature of the surface being measured. Where inaccuracies do occur as a result of a wrongly set emissivity value, these will only affect the accuracy of the temperature reading. The amount of change and the rate of change in the temperature will still be measured precisely.

6.5 *Infra-red thermography*

A useful method for measuring the temperature remotely is by means of a thermal imager. This has become more common in recent years as the devices have become more affordable. Thermal imagers are not ordinarily considered to be thermometers; however, they can be used to provide accurate and precise measurements of temperature. They operate in a similar manner to infra-red thermometers, using the thermal (infra-red) energy emitted from an object in order to determine its temperature. To ensure the greatest accuracy the user may need to pre-enter an emissivity value for different objects and materials that are being measured and thermal imaging cannot be used to measure the temperature of the air.

Thermal imagers are able to present the investigator with the temperature information in two ways; by displaying the temperature as a numerical value and also by means of a thermograph, which is a pictorial representation of the area being measured. A thermograph is similar to a photograph, but instead of light, it uses the thermal energy that is emitted by objects and surfaces to create a visual representation of the scene.

The visual presentation of the data can cause some investigators to consider the thermographic image in the same way as an ordinary photograph. This misunderstanding sometimes causes them to mistakenly think that some of their thermographs contain unusual or interesting visual anomalies. For example, the infra-red lighting that is used with night vision cameras may occasionally be reflected off some surfaces or objects, this can result in the appearance of anomalies within the image or cause unexpected temperature values to be displayed. Investigators who regularly use a thermal imager in proximity with night vision cameras and infra-red lights should be aware of this potential problem.

Using a thermal imager in order to measure the temperature may offer the investigator several significant advantages: They react very quickly to temperature change, and because the user can see the precise area being measured, they offer a greater degree of measuring precision than ordinary non-contact thermometers. The area being measured may be fixed or it may be selectable by the user. Thermal cameras have a high thermal sensitivity, typically better than 0.1° Celsius and a sampling rate of between five and fifteen times per second. An accuracy of less than +/-2% of the indicated value should be expected.

All thermal imagers can store their data for later review and analysis using software, which is normally provided free by the manufacturer. Using the software, the investigator can examine each of the individual temperature measuring points in every thermograph (radiometric jpeg). Depending upon the model, each thermograph can contain between 4800 and 76,800 measuring points (even more, with expensive scientific and industrial thermal imagers). The data from the individual measuring points can also be used for making detailed radiometric measurements of the overall scene.

A number of thermography training courses are available and investigators who regularly use thermal imaging may find it beneficial to undertake one of these courses; most are available online, sometimes for little or no cost.

7 | Measuring the Temperature

As with any system of measurement, the accuracy and precision of temperature data is governed not only by the equipment that is used, but to a great extent by the methods that were used to obtain the measurements.

It is important to appreciate that any thermometer, however accurate, is only capable of measuring the temperature of a small area. This will be either the region immediately surrounding the sensor or which lies within the sensor's field of view. Significant temperature variations are likely to exist elsewhere within the same room or space and the small area that is being measured may not accurately represent the entire space.

Walking around a location searching for unusual temperature readings, or placing the thermometer onto the nearest convenient surface will in all likelihood result in the investigator having a very poor understanding of the temperature; how it is changing or what may be causing those changes. Temperature measurements need to be undertaken with an understanding of how the local environment can cause significant variations in the temperature to occur. The air inside a building is constantly moving, mixing warm and cooler air. The movement of people and the opening and closing of doors will exacerbate this motion. In addition to the obvious sources such as heaters and air conditioning, there will be some degree of heating and cooling of the air caused by the surfaces it is in contact with. These influences may sometimes be subtle and difficult to discern, nevertheless the investigator should always seek an explanation for any temperature measurement that appears to be unusual or unexpected. The investigator should also not overlook the outside weather and how the prevailing conditions can affect the micro climate inside the location. The direction and strength of the wind may significantly change the interior air flow, and exterior walls that are wet due to rain may be measurably cooler than when they are dry. The temperature inside a building is also affected by the residual heat retained by the structure and the materials that have been used. Poor or defective insulation may cause the temperature to alter more rapidly than in areas with better insulation.

The frequency at which temperature measurements are made is also an important consideration. Normally, the investigator will be guided by previously reported temperature experiences of witnesses. In situations where the temperature appears to be changing rapidly, it may be advantageous to record the temperature every one or two minutes.

At other times, when the temperature appears more stable, updating the temperature data once every fifteen minutes might suffice. The measuring frequency should be flexibly altered in response to changes in the observed temperature or reports of perceived temperature change. If it is necessary or desirous to record the temperature more frequently, e.g., more than once every fifteen minutes, then the use of an automated data-logging thermometer is advised. If the temperature is being recorded manually, this may be simplified by using a prepared chart with additional space for also documenting the location and time of each measurement.

7.1 *Baseline measurements*

It is often helpful for the investigator to make a continuous series of temperature measurements within a particular room or location. This not only provides a point of reference for all of their subsequent measurements but it can also be used to indicate general temperature trends over a period of time. (also **see Sec. 2.5**)

Using a data-logging thermometer is recommended. This needs to be placed centrally (horizontally and vertically) within the space and away from any obvious sources of heat or draughts of air. Avoid placing the sensor onto the floor or in close proximity to any surfaces which may unduly affect the measurements. With thermometers that have an internal sensor, attaching it to a tripod or stand may be helpful. For devices which have a sensor on the end of a length of wire, the sensor can sometimes be attached to a conveniently located video camera tripod, ensuring that it is well away from any heat produced by the camera. Attaching the sensor to a short length of garden cane, is another simple method of raising the sensor height; the base of the cane can be temporarily secured using tape, blu-tac or plasticine.

Measurements should be taken at regular intervals throughout the visit. In the majority of situations, it will normally be sufficient to record the temperature once every ten to fifteen minutes. If a data-logging thermometer is used, then increasing the frequency of the measurements may be worthwhile in order to show the temperature fluctuations in greater detail.

7.2 *Using multiple thermometers*

Using several thermometers is often a helpful and practical means of measuring the temperature in different parts of the location or at different points within the same room or space. Compared to other items of paranormal investigation equipment, thermometers are inexpensive and it is recommended that investigators equip themselves with several thermometers. For team investigations, it may also be helpful to encourage every member to have a thermometer available for use, if required.

7.3 *Calibrating multiple thermometers*

Whenever the investigator uses multiple thermometers, even if they are identical models, it is likely that they will notice small differences in the measured values shown on the devices. These differences are perfectly normal and are due to variations in the components and the specified tolerance of individual thermometers or they may come about due to the way in which the temperature is measured. The specification sheet supplied with each thermometer will normally include information about the accuracy of the device. This is often stated as a percentage of the displayed value or in degrees, sometimes both. For example, if the specified accuracy of two thermometers is given as being plus or minus 1°C, then it is perfectly normal for there to be up to a 2°C difference in the indicated temperatures when the two devices are being used to measure the same temperature.

7.3.1 *Comparative calibration*

Investigators who use several thermometers may find it is helpful to carry out a basic comparative calibration step in order to allow the data from different thermometers to be more easily compared. Comparative calibration is a straightforward procedure which the investigator should repeat periodically, once or twice each year. The only items that are required, are a closable cardboard or plastic box, large enough to hold all of the thermometers and some means of labelling or numbering the individual thermometers.

- Nominate one of the thermometers to be the master device.

Label this as the master thermometer or number one. Label or number the rest of the thermometers in turn.

- Turn on all of the devices and ensure that are all set to the same unit of measurement. Place them into the closed box and put the box in a normally heated room.

- Wait for a minimum of five to ten minutes for the sensors to become stabilised. Immediately upon opening the box, make a note of the temperature shown on every thermometer.

- The difference between the temperature indicated on the master thermometer and that shown on each of the remaining thermometers can then be used to quickly calculate the amount of correction necessary to directly comparing their measurements with those of the master thermometer or against one another.

  For example, assuming the master thermometer indicates a measurement of 20°. If the displayed value on thermometer #2 is 21° then a SUBTRACTION of 1° should be applied to all subsequent measurements taken with that thermometer. If thermometer #3 shows a value of 18.5° then a correction of 1.5° should be ADDED to all subsequent measurements with that thermometer.

- Determine the correction value for all of the devices in turn. The master thermometer needs NO CORRECTION to be applied to its measurements.

- The subtraction or addition value for each individual thermometer should be recorded, e.g., + 1.5, - 0.7 etc., and marked onto the thermometer itself using either a label or a permanent marker pen.

For those wishing to make their temperature measurements even more accurate, they may decide to undertake a three-zone calibration procedure. This uses the same technique described above but it is repeated three times using three different temperature zones.

- Place the boxed thermometers into a cold space such as a refrigerator. Note the indicated measurements on each thermometer. Repeat, with the boxed thermometers placed in a normally heated room and again note the measurements. Lastly, place the boxed thermometers into a warm space, such as an airing cupboard and note the final set of measurements.

- Calculate the correction that is needed for each thermometer in the three different temperature zones (cold, normal and warm). It may be noticed that sometimes a thermometer will require different amounts of correction to be applied in the different temperature zones. However, it is sufficient to use an average of the three correction values in order to provide the overall correction factor for each thermometer.

  For example, when compared against the temperature shown on the master thermometer, if thermometer #2 reads +1° in the cold zone, +0.5° at room temperature and +1.4° in the warm zone, then a SUBTRACTION of 0.96° [1 + 0.5 + 1.4 = 2.9 / 3] should be applied to all of the subsequent measurements. For convenience, this may be rounded to - 1° and marked on the device.

  If thermometer #3, reads of +1° in the cold zone, - 1.5° at room temperature and -1° in the warm zone then a correction of 0.5° [1 + (-1.5) + (-1) = (-1.5) / 3] should be ADDED to all of the subsequent measurements and a correction value of + 0.5 marked onto the device.

7.4 *Set the emissivity*

Prior to using a non-contact or thermal imager for measuring the temperature it is helpful to set the correct emissivity prior to use. Doing so will increase the accuracy of the measurements. In situations where an object's emissivity is not known or when a wide range of surface finishes are present an emissivity value of 0.95 should be used. The same emissivity value should be used by any other non-contact thermometer which is being used in the same room or space. It may be necessary to change the emissivity setting on each thermometer if they are subsequently used elsewhere in the location.

The emissivity value used should be recorded in the investigation report in order that any subsequent investigation is able to use the same emissivity value and directly compare the measurements. (also **see Sec. 6.4**)

7.5 *Ambient (air) temperature*

Using a single temperature measuring point can rarely provide a true representation of the ambient air temperature throughout an entire room or space. However, the investigator may occasionally only require a general indication of the temperature. In this instance, positioning the thermometer in the middle of the space, in a similar manner to that which is used when making a baseline measurement may be acceptable.

In order to gain a more representative value of the ambient temperature in a room or space, it is necessary for the investigator to make a series of measurements at several points spaced evenly throughout the room at the mid-point between floor and ceiling. Ordinarily, the spacing between individual measuring points should be around one or two metres. The number of measuring points may be increased if the investigator suspects that there is a lot of temperature variability in the space that is being measured. For even greater accuracy, each measuring point, can be further divided into three additional measurement levels. These should be at 20 to 30cm above the floor, mid-way between floor and ceiling and 20 to 30cm below the ceiling. However, this process is time consuming and will only be required in those cases where a temperature anomaly is suspected or reported and when the investigator is seeking the greatest amount of data in order to assist them.

In order to more accurately account for any temperature variations which might occur during the time taken to complete the measurements, it is recommended that they be done using several thermometers simultaneously. It is just about possible to make a series of measurements throughout a space using a single thermometer, but this will unlikely to properly take account of any temperature variations that occur during the measuring process.

Once the measurements are completed, the data can then be used to determine an average value for the entire space by simply adding together all of the individual measurements to give a sum total, then dividing this figure by the number of measuring points. The individual measurements from the different points can be also used to indicate areas where temperature variations exist. The investigator may then examine these either visually or by making further measurements. In some instances, the investigator may decide to use a different method of examining the area such as using a thermal imager in order to try and determine the cause or source.

7.6 *Verifying reports of feeling colder (or warmer)*

The investigator must always consider measuring the temperature in any circumstance in which an individual reports an unexpected or unusual temperature variation. Some of these reports may be due to the witness having the sensation of a temperature change when no actual variation in the ambient temperature took place, whilst other reports may be caused by an actual change in the temperature. Only by carefully measuring the temperature within the area indicated by the reports can the investigator attempt to ascertain the actuality and the extent of any reported environmental temperature variations.

Taking one or two snap-shot measurements of a person's temperature is unlikely to reveal very much information of value for the investigator. Their temperature may indeed be measurably lower or higher than expected and there are many perfectly ordinary reasons for this to be the case. It is normal to find that extremities such as the head, hands and feet may be markedly cooler or warmer than other areas of the body. Sometimes, the reason for these variations may be straightforward; the individual might have been sitting in a cold draught or may have recently had a hot drink. At other times, the cause may not be quite so apparent. Skin temperature is directly affected by the amount of blood flowing through the upper layers of the skin. This blood flow can alter in response to an individual's emotional state or as a result from them consuming alcohol and tobacco. Some medical conditions too, which the person may or may not be aware that they have e.g., Raynaud's syndrome, can also cause their skin temperature to change rapidly.

Ordinarily, without carrying out an extensive and invasive series of measurements it is difficult to know what a person's normal temperature range will be. It may be worthwhile placing a thermometer into very close contact with the person for a period of time. This can be achieved by attaching the sensor of a data-logging thermometer to the outside of the person's clothing; the tip of a shoulder is a convenient and unobtrusive location to attach the sensor. A series of measurements carried out in this way may sometimes illicit information about the changes in the temperature which the person is describing. However, measuring the temperature in close proximity to a person will inevitably result in the data being affected by their body heat although this will only affect the overall accuracy of the data, the precision of the measurements will be unaltered.

A non-contact thermometer may also prove worthwhile, especially in instances where it is not practical or unwise to use an attached thermometer sensor. To improve the accuracy of this method, measurements should be obtained in close proximity (within six or eight inches) of the person, in order to properly align the thermometer's field of view. Occasionally, differences between the emissivity value of the person's clothing and their skin may significantly affect the accuracy of the measurements.

If one is available, a thermal imager is the possibly the most useful and least invasive means of non-invasively determining a person's temperature. Obtaining a series of thermographs at intervals will permit the temperature of the person and also of their immediate surroundings to be obtained without requiring close contact with the person and with a high degree of accuracy. Thermal imaging also allows the investigator to quickly determine the temperature of different regions of the body.

7.7 *Other temperature measurements*

Investigators will occasionally need to measure the temperature of an object or structure. This may be to locate sources of heating or cooling or when measurements of the ambient temperature reveal an area in which the temperature is higher or lower than the investigator might reasonably expect.

In these situations, it may be helpful to use a non-contact thermometer. Slowly scan the thermometer across each surface or object in turn, observing for any significant variations in the surface temperature which could be affecting the temperature of the surrounding air.

To obtain a higher degree of accuracy, the investigator may alter the emissivity value used by the thermometer. In situations where the objects to be checked are comprised of different materials and surface finishes, selecting an average emissivity value of 0.95 is advised. If a surface of interest is identified, it may then be examined to try to determine the cause of the temperature reading. Sometimes, there may be a seemingly obvious likely source, such as a window, air vent or doorway, but it is important to avoid any assumptions being made. In every instance, the investigator must check even the most obvious potential source in order to ascertain that it is the actual cause.

In situations where a cause is not immediately apparent,

thermography can be advantageous. It is a reliable way of revealing hidden sources of temperature variations, such as enclosed or embedded pipework or inefficient insulation. Draughts and other air leaks will also often reveal themselves as a slight change in the temperature of nearby surfaces which a thermal imager can quickly indicate. Analysis of the thermographs may reveal further information about the nature of the temperature variation and its source.

7.8 *Precautions and care*

Thermometers, like every other item of equipment, can occasionally malfunction. For example, several models of non-contact thermometer are known to suddenly start giving unusually low or high measurements when their battery begins to run low and before any low-battery warning appears in the display. If an unexpected or unusual measurement is observed, it is important that it is verified, which can be quickly done using a second thermometer. This also serves to check and ensure the accuracy of the initial measurement and eliminate any erroneous data. Should a thermometer appear to be malfunctioning then it should be immediately withdrawn from use until it can be demonstrated to be working correctly.

Some temperature sensors, notably those which consist of an exposed electronic component, are susceptible to humidity and dampness. It is important to store these devices in a dry environment and to allow sufficient time for the sensor to acclimatise when moving them between different environments in order to prevent condensation from affecting their operation and causing them to mis-read. Some temperature sensors are sensitive to physical damage caused by mishandling. If a protective cover is supplied by the manufacturer, it should always be fitted when the device is not in use. The investigator should also remember to check that the cover is removed prior to use.

Non-contact thermometers and thermal imagers will give an incorrect measurement value if the sensor's field of view is even partially obscured. Care should be taken to ensure that fingers or other items such as protective covers do not obscure the sensor when measurements are being made. This is more likely to happen with non-contact thermometers as any obstruction will usually be apparent on the viewing screen of a thermal imager.

All non-contact thermometers have a simple focussing lens in front of the infra-red sensor; typically, this will be made from translucent plastic. This lens should be inspected prior to each use and kept clean. The lens is normally rugged enough to be cleaned using a soft cloth or tissue to remove any dirt, moisture or debris that has accumulated. Thermal imagers also require a lens in order to accurately focus the thermal emissions onto the sensor. The lens of a thermal imager is made from a special type of coated glass or optical crystal. The lens material and the coating are easily damaged and must only be cleaned using high quality camera lens cleaning materials following the recommendations of the manufacturer.

Thermal imagers, require a period of sensor self-calibration before they can be used to make measurements. The device will normally indicate when these are complete and the device is ready to be used.

8 | Weather and Local Atmospheric Conditions

Many investigators overlook the value of observing and recording the local prevailing weather conditions during an investigation. However, the weather may be a significant factor in some cases. For example, in windy conditions there is an increased likelihood of interior draughts being felt and internal pressure variations between the upwind and leeward side of a building can cause the structure to flex noisily and doors to move.

In cold weather the use of heating appliances can result in unexpected operating sounds and air currents created by differential thermal gradients.

The weather can also act in more subtle ways. The wind moving through and around structures may create unusual sound effects. It can also produce low frequency infrasound. Infrasound cannot be heard, but it can have an unsettling effect on some individuals, causing them to report a range of unusual psycho-physiological sensations. A regional zone of high pressure, normally indicated by fine and settled weather, alters the way in which radio waves are propagated, leading to unusual radio interference or the reception of signals and voices not normally heard by those undertaking EVP radio experiments.

8.1 *Measuring the weather*

In the majority of cases, the investigator may check one of the official weather forecasts that are available. However, some of these forecasts may not accurately reflect the weather at the location being investigated. Weather reports are compiled using data from a series of Met Office weather stations around the country, the nearest of which may be some distance from the investigation site and the reported data might be different from the prevailing local conditions. In these circumstances, the investigator might search for one of an increasing number of local weather stations that are maintained by amateur enthusiasts or local agencies. Alternatively, they may wish to make their own on-site observations.

Measurements of the outside temperature can be undertaken using a simple analogue garden thermometer and an inexpensive anemometer can be used to measure the windspeed. In some situations, particularly those in which the investigator suspects that the prevailing weather may be significant, it is helpful to gather weather data from each of the exposed sides of the location in order to record any variations which may be due to the direction of the prevailing weather. The weather should be recorded at the start of the investigation session and updated at regular intervals throughout. Note the outside temperature, the prevailing conditions, e.g., rain, fog etc., the wind speed and direction and any other information that is considered to be relevant.

8.2 *Humidity, dew Point and air pressure*

The investigator may sometimes consider making other observations pertaining to the prevailing local atmospheric conditions including making measurements of the humidity, dew point and air pressure. There are a number of researchers who have suggested or speculated that examining these variables may be helpful. Condensation which forms when ambient conditions permit can occasionally lead to reports of ethereal misty figures being seen or captured on camera. When the air is dry, it can facilitate the build-up of electrostatic charges causing some people to experience unusual physical sensations, others may describe headaches, feelings of malaise and occasionally even visual disturbances.

Devices that combine several types of measuring instrument into a single unit have become commonplace and all of these environmental variables which may not have been previously considered or measured by investigators can now be easily measured and examined in some detail.

8.2.1 *Humidity*

Humidity is an indication of the amount of water vapour that is suspended in the air. It can be expressed in several ways; as absolute humidity (AH), which is the total amount of water contained within a given volume of air, specific humidity (SH), which is the ratio between a volume of air and the water contained within it and relative humidity (RH) that is the percentage of water contained within a given volume of air. Relative humidity is the most commonly used means of expressing the ambient humidity.

The amount of water which can be contained within any volume of air is directly related to the temperature of the air. Warmer air can hold greater amounts of water than cooler air. Therefore, in order to be meaningful, every measurement of relative humidity must always include the ambient air temperature, obtained at the same time.

Hygrometers, which measure relative humidity, are often combined with thermometers in the form of a dual measuring instrument called a thermo-hygrometer. Relative humidity is rarely considered to be an important metric for the investigator. However, in some situations, measuring the relative humidity may prove to be helpful. For example, changes in the ambient humidity can affect the body's normal processes of temperature regulation and the way in which individuals perceive and report the ambient temperature.

8.2.2 *Dew point and condensation*

Closely linked to the humidity is the dew point. This is the temperature at which the water held within the air begins to condense and form droplets on surfaces. Close to the dew point, mist and fog can form. In some instances, this has been known to be the cause of apparitional reports and the appearance of unusual mists. Dew point is always expressed as a temperature value. It is calculated from knowing the air temperature and the relative humidity. Many thermo-hygrometers have an option to calculate and display the dew point.

Breath condensation is also linked to humidity and temperature, although its occurrence is more difficult to predict as it is affected by other factors including the temperature and the humidity of the exhaled air. As a rough guide, an average adult should not be surprised to observe condensation in their exhaled breath at ambient air temperatures of 10°C and below.

8.2.3 *Air pressure*

Air pressure is another potentially useful way in which the ambient atmosphere at a location may be understood. Air pressure, the force which the atmospheric air mass exerts on an object, is normally measured using the SI unit of hectopascals (hPa). Although some agencies and services still express air pressure by means of other recognised standards, including millibars (mb), millimetres of mercury (mmHG) or atmospheres (atm).

Air pressure varies constantly and is affected by changes in air temperature, relative humidity, altitude and also by the movement of air. The air pressure at a location may alter in two distinct ways:

- Gradual variations which tend to take place slowly over time, as a result of passing weather systems. Ordinarily, these weather-related changes are of less interest to investigators as they tend to act uniformly inside and outside over a wide area. Changes in the air pressure may sometimes cause physical effects. For example, instances of low atmospheric air pressure can cause changes in the level of the ground water table, which may lead to pooling or more rarely lead to flooding in basements and other low-lying areas.

- Smaller pressure fluctuations also exist, and these are potentially of much greater interest to investigators. Typically, these small variations, often less than 0.10hPa, can happen suddenly or they may occur many times every minute. They are caused by localised air movement, e.g., wind gusts or air leakage, the opening of doors and windows and other human actions and activities. Although these changes in the air pressure are small, their effects can often be readily apparent, especially indoors, where they are often sufficient to create unexpected draughts or cause doors to move without any apparent intervention. It is also known that rapid changes in air pressure can cause a structure to flex or move slightly thereby producing unexpected sounds and noises as a result.

Air pressure is measured using a barometer. Barometers are often included in weather measuring instruments. However, barometers designed for weather observations are not capable of measuring small fluctuations in air pressure as they are primarily designed to measure those more gradual pressure variations caused by the passage of weather systems.

Nowadays, a barometer is often built into smartphones, tablet computers and activity tracking devices. The internal barometers that are used in these devices are extremely sensitive; some are capable of detecting pressure changes of less than 0.01 hPa. Many of these devices allow the user to directly access the output of the barometer and record the air pressure data directly to the device itself. This data can be downloaded afterwards in order to produce a record of air pressure changes over a longer period of time. Some barometer Apps which are intended for weather observation may have a long interval between samples; these particular Apps may be unable to detect and record small rapid fluctuations in the air pressure.

8.3 *Measuring humidity, dew point and air pressure*

The majority of these measurements can easily be automated and the individual recordings time indexed. Several devices are available in which the measurements of humidity, dew point, air pressure and thermometer are combined into a single piece of equipment that once set-up, can be placed in a suitable location and left unattended.

A single combination device used in this way will usually suffice for obtaining a baseline series of measurements, against which other measurements can be compared. When selecting the location to place a single combination device, the investigator should prioritise for measuring the temperature. The rationale for this is twofold; firstly, temperature is generally more likely to be of interest and secondly, humidity and pressure variations tend to affect a wider area and any inaccuracies with the data for these variables is likely to be less significant. If the investigator wishes only to obtain a reasonably accurate baseline, placing the device centrally (horizontally and vertically) in a room or space is suggested. It is recommended that a separate device is used for each individual room or space.

8.4 *Air movement*

It is virtually never the case that the air inside a location is perfectly still. Small temperature and pressure variations, draughts and even the movement of the people will all create small but nonetheless significant and measurable movements of the air. Occasionally, these subtle motions of the air, pushing upon a large surface area, e.g., a door, are sufficient to cause it to move, but more often a witness will describe feeling these gentle air movements on exposed skin. They are common enough to be referred to as 'psychic breezes' by some investigators.

The movement of air is measured using an anemometer. Traditional anemometers use some form of rotating turbine, consisting of either a series of blades or cups, to convert the spinning motion into a measurement of the air's velocity. However, this design is unsuitable for use indoors where the speed of the moving air is much lower. Interior air motion is best measured by using a hot-wire anemometer, which uses a very fine wire element made from a metal that alters its electrical characteristics depending upon its temperature. The air moving past the wire has a cooling effect on the wire and the electrical properties of the wire are altered. A measuring circuit is then used to determine the velocity of the air. The method is highly accurate and is capable of measuring even extremely low air speeds.

The SI unit for measuring the movement of air is metres per second (m/s). Using this scale provides a convenient way for the investigator to directly compare measurements made inside or outside of the location. There are also several other established units that are also in regular use, e.g., knots (nautical miles per hour) or the Beaufort scale (expressed as a numerical scale from 1 - 12). Using the Beaufort scale is not recommended as it only gives a general indication of the wind strength, rather than a direct measurement of the actual speed.

To ensure that the measurements are of the greatest accuracy, the anemometer must be aligned with the direction of the air's movement. Outside, this is normally quite an easy matter. Indoors, the subtle air motion may be harder to discern and it may be necessary for the investigator to slowly orientate the anemometer until the highest value is observed; this which will normally indicate the main direction of the air's movement. Some hot-wire and rotating turbine anemometers have a provision for recording and time-stamping the measurements, but many need to be read manually and the information recorded within the investigation notes; this record should also include the location and the time each measurement was made.

9 | Electromagnetic Fields

As the name indicates, an electromagnetic field consists of two components; an electric field and a magnetic field. An electric field surrounds every electrically charged particle, it can also be generated by a changing magnetic field. A magnetic field surrounds any intrinsically magnetic material, it can also be generated by a changing electric field.

In an electromagnetic field, the two fields are intrinsically interrelated. Any amount of change in one will always cause a change to take place within the other.

The polarization (orientation) of the electromagnetic field is always determined by the motion of the electric charge. The intensity of an electromagnetic field changes proportionally as the distance from its source is increased or decreased; for example, if the distance from the source is doubled, its intensity is normally reduced to one quarter of the initial value. The intensity of the field can also be affected by the materials that it passes through or by interactions with them. It can be reflected or attenuated, creating localised regions in which the measured intensity may be significantly higher or lower than that which may ordinarily be expected.

An electromagnetic field (wave) may be described in several ways: By reference to its frequency, which is normally expressed using units of Hertz (Hz); its wavelength, normally expressed using metric units of measurement (centimetres, metres and kilometres), or by referring to its properties (radio, light, heat, etc).

The electromagnetic spectrum extends from frequencies which are significantly below 1Hz with corresponding wavelengths that are measured in thousands of kilometres, to frequencies in excess of 10^{20} Hz with wavelengths in the sub atomic range.

Electromagnetic fields can be man-made or they may occur naturally. Man-made sources include any electrical appliance or device, radio transmitters, the electrical wiring inside buildings and electricity supply cables. Electromagnetic fields can also exist around metal objects such as metal water pipes and the metal framework of buildings. Natural sources are primarily the Earth's (geo)magnetic field, the Sun, seismic activity, lightning and the movement of air and water within the atmosphere. Humans and other living organisms also produce an electromagnetic field around them as a result of the electrical activity that occurs within their cells.

9.1 *Choosing an EMF meter*

Many of the devices which are used by investigators including thermometers, cameras, thermal imagers and light sensors, operate by recording or measuring some part of the electromagnetic spectrum. In this section we will only consider those devices that are specifically designed for measuring electromagnetic fields that have a frequency range of between 3Hz and 30GHz. This region lies within the radio frequency (RF) portion of the electromagnetic spectrum and incorporates electromagnetic fields that occur naturally and also those which are produced by man-made sources.

Electromagnetic fields in this range are normally measured using some type of electromagnetic field meter, normally referred to as an EMF meter by investigators.

The use of EMF meters by investigators is supported by innumerable ideas, notions and theories, including suggestions that ghosts and spirits emit electromagnetism by which they can be detected or that they can manipulate it as a means of communicating with the living. Others propose that exposure of the brain to electromagnetism is a significant cause for a range of reported paranormal experiences. Much of the research that indicates a possible link between reported paranormal experiences and electromagnetic fields has been conducted at frequencies below 100Hz and there is little to suggest that meters which operate significantly above this range can provide any worthwhile data for investigators. Nevertheless, the wealth of ideas and opinion has resulted in electromagnetic fields becoming the most commonly observed and measured physical variable by investigators of paranormal phenomena.

EMF measuring devices currently being used by investigators range from simple models that provide the user with only an indication of the electromagnetic field strength, up to models which allow accurate measurements to be made of a field's intensity and its frequency. In addition, EMF detecting devices are also used by investigators who are attempting to communicate with, or detect the presence of, ghosts, spirits and other entities. Some purpose-built ghost hunting items, contain a simple EMF sensing circuit; these include a number of soft toys that are intended to be used as trigger objects.

In many instances, the devices that are being used were originally designed for use by individuals with health and well-being concerns as a result of their exposure to man-made electromagnetic fields. Depending upon the model, most of these are intended to detect or measure electromagnetic fields between 20Hz and 10GHz. Typically, these models will have a single-axis sensor that responds to the magnetic component of an electromagnetic field. Measurements (if they are provided) are expressed using units of magnetic field intensity, e.g., milliGauss or MicroTesla. A few devices also include a separate sensor for measuring the electric field; this is normally expressed in units of Volts/metre.

9.2 *Single-axis or three-axis?*

The majority of EMF meters used by investigators have a sensor that is sensitive in only one direction. This is determined by the physical orientation of the sensor within the device. The orientation of the sensor and its position may be marked onto the exterior of the device or in the instructions. Some meters fail to indicate the orientation of their sensor, in which case it is usual to assume that the sensor's orientation will be the same as the longest physical dimension of the meter. Unfortunately, not every device will use this arrangement and the investigator may need to experiment in order to determine the sensor's orientation. It is recommended to avoid any meter which does not properly indicate the orientation of the sensor as this is important information for the user.

Unless the orientation of the sensor is properly aligned with the polarization of the electromagnetic field, significant measuring errors will occur. With any single-axis device the sensor must be aligned before any measurements are made (**see Sec. 10.1**).

In order to improve the accuracy of their measurements, investigators should consider using a three-axis (triaxial) meter whenever possible. Meters of this type have either a single three-axis sensor, or three single-axis sensors which are set at right angles to the one another. Triaxial meters are capable of measuring the intensity of the field, without the user needing to align the sensor.

The position and orientation of the sensor/s is usually indicated on the device or in the user manual. The orientation of the three measurement axes is normally labelled as the X-axis, Y-axis and Z-axis. Most devices will allow the user to choose how the measurements are presented; either as the combined sum of all three axes (overall field intensity), or the value of each axis separately (useful for determining the field's polarization).

Three axis designs are typically more expensive than single-axis models. However, the additional cost may be justified by their greater precision, ease of use and the time-saving that can be expected when using this type of meter. For investigators wishing to measure the electromagnetic fields over an extended period of time, a number of three-axis EMF data-logging devices are available.

9.3 *The importance of frequency*

Every electromagnetic field has two defining characteristics; its amplitude, which describes the strength of the field, and its frequency which is the number of oscillations per second of the field. One of the most significant problems when carrying out electromagnetic field measurements is that the majority of EMF meters that are used by investigators only provide amplitude information. Amplitude measurements may be helpful when the investigator wishes to assess the overall strength of the electromagnetic fields at an investigation site. However, using a device that only indicates the amplitude offers the investigator almost no information about the nature of the electromagnetic field they are measuring and even less about its source.

The frequency of an electromagnetic field may be likened to its fingerprint. Knowing the frequency of an electromagnetic field allows the investigator to determine its likely cause. Almost the entire radio frequency spectrum is strictly controlled. Frequencies are allocated and regulated by official agencies all around the World. Detailed frequency plans are readily available from a number of official and independent sources, e.g., Ofcom in the UK and the FCC in the USA. A number of these resources also offer precise geographic and user information relating to each specific frequency. By this means, it is often a straightforward matter for the investigator to draw up a list of potential sources. These can then be checked in turn, making additional measurements and observations if necessary, in order to locate the actual or the most likely source of any detected electromagnetic field.

There are a number of EMF meters available which provide the user with both the amplitude and the frequency of a measured electromagnetic field. These cost only a little more than the price of a good quality amplitude-only EMF meter. For investigators who wish to carry out a comprehensive study of the electromagnetism at a location, or who wish to state with a greater degree of certainty the source of any detected electromagnetic field, these meters provide a significant advantage. Therefore, it may be prudent for investigators to consider obtaining just one or two amplitude and frequency EMF meters, instead of buying several amplitude-only devices.

9.4 *EMF meter frequency range and selectivity*

EMF meter manufacturers will normally specify the range of frequencies at which their device is most sensitive and accurate. The operating range is often determined by the device's intended use. For example, meters intended for making general measurements within the home or workplace are designed to be most sensitive when used for measuring frequencies around the electricity supply frequency of 50Hz (60Hz in the USA). Whereas meters intended for detecting microwave-oven door leakage or cellular communications will typically have their greatest sensitivity at around 1 to 3 GHz.

Some manufacturers may describe their device as being capable of detecting and measuring a wide range of frequencies, e.g., from 20Hz to 2GHz. In many instances, the sensitivity and accuracy of these models will not be uniform across the entire frequency range. In some models, this will result in a significant decrease in the accuracy of some of the measurements. Depending upon the frequency of the field, these devices can under-read by as much as 75% of the actual field strength, which is of little help for investigators wishing to determine the actual levels of the ambient electromagnetism.

Meters which have a narrow frequency range are preferred and will usually be considerably more accurate than those with a broader operating range. Users should also seek EMF meters that provide a high level of selectivity. This is the ability of the device to reject unwanted electromagnetic frequencies which may interfere with the accuracy of the measurements. Selectivity is normally expressed as a ratio using units of decibels (dB); the higher this ratio, the better the device will be at rejecting unwanted interference. Manufacturers may incorporate filtering circuits into the design in order to reduce the interference and minimise erroneous measurements caused by unwanted fields.

Filter circuits add additional cost but their inclusion significantly improves the selectivity and the accuracy of the meter.

9.5 *Testing the EMF meter*

It is recommended that investigators take some time to acquaint themselves with their EMF meter before it is used on any investigation, in order for them to become familiar with the responses of their meter at different frequencies and to check that it is operating correctly. This can easily be done using known sources of electromagnetism. For those wishing to do this, there are a number of easily accessible and readily available sources of different electromagnetic frequency ranges. These include the electricity supply and electrical appliances (50Hz or 60Hz), walkie-talkie radios (normally around 450Hz) and WIFI routers (usually 2.4 or 5 GHz). Ordinarily, one should avoid using televisions, personal computers and lighting systems for these tests as some of these appliances e.g., low wattage compact fluorescent lightbulbs (CFLs) and video screens, can also emit electromagnetic fields that are significantly higher than the electricity supply frequency.

9.6 *EMF emitting devices*

There are a number of ghost hunting devices on the market that are designed to emit an electromagnetic field. These devices, which are increasingly popular, are inspired by the same ideas and notions that have led to the widespread use of EMF measuring devices. However, instead of detecting the ambient electromagnetism that is supposedly used by spirits and other entities, these devices are promoted as being able to facilitate or improve spirit manifestations, by supplying them with additional electromagnetic energy.

Various methods to achieve this are used in these devices; some have rotating magnets whilst others have a varying electric current passing through a coil of wire. Neither method is able to generate an electromagnetic field of any significant amplitude and none have been shown to offer the investigator any worthwhile advantage; their use cannot be recommended.

10 | Using an EMF Meter

The majority of the EMF meters used by investigators are designed for handheld use and it is common practise for the investigator to walk around the location, holding the meter and observing the readout. Unfortunately, doing so will significantly increase the likelihood of measuring errors being produced. Handholding the meter inevitably places it close to the investigator's body and also to other devices they may be carrying, e.g., a radio, camera, smartphone etc. When using an EMF meter in this manner, it is advisable to always hold it at arm's length and ensure that any nearby electrical devices are either switched off or kept well away from the meter whilst undertaking measurements.

Moving the meter around whilst searching for, or measuring, an electromagnetic field can significantly increase the likelihood of an erroneous measurement. Many simple EMF meters will over-read whenever the meter is moved through an electromagnetic field (or through a magnetic field); the more rapidly the meter is moved, the higher will be the indicated value (**see Sec. 9.0**). A similar situation can occur when using a meter that is primarily intended for measuring the electrical power supply, which has a frequency of 50Hz or 60Hz. The sensitivity of the meter may extend some-way below this frequency and moving the meter may cause it to respond to the Earth's geomagnetic field.

Movements, where necessary, should be always be made slowly, maintaining the same orientation of the meter throughout. To ensure the greatest accuracy, it is recommended that the meter should be held still whilst the measurement is being made.

10.1 *Aligning a single-axis sensor*

Whenever a single-axis sensor is used, failing to properly align the sensor with the polarization of the electromagnetic field will cause the measurements to be significantly lower than the field's actual intensity. The position of the sensor and the orientation of its measuring axis will normally be indicated somewhere on the body of the device or within the instruction manual.

In many instances, especially at the commencement of the investigation, the polarization of the electromagnetic fields will not be known. In these circumstances, the following method can be used to align the sensor with the polarization of the field; it may also be helpful if the investigator wishes to simply determine the polarization of a detected electromagnetic field.

- Start by holding the meter away from the user's body, parallel to the floor with the display uppermost. Then slowly rotate <u>and</u> tilt the meter approximately 90° in every direction until the highest reading is observed. This indicates that the meter is closely aligned with the electromagnetic field. Note: This alignment procedure will need to be repeated for every measurement.

- To determine the maximum intensity of the field it is then a simple matter of holding the meter in its new orientation whilst moving it forwards and backwards, side to side or up and down until the highest reading is seen. When no further increase in the electromagnetic level is observed, the measurement can be made and the measuring position noted. Investigators may also wish to note the polarization of the field on a plan or diagram of the area or location which they are examining.

10.2 *Alternative methods for aligning the sensor*

Sometimes, the investigator may wish to make measurements for an extended period or there may be occasions when it is impractical for them to handhold the meter. In these circumstances, they may decide that it is preferable or more convenient to simply place the meter onto a table or some other surface. However, when a single-axis EMF meter is used in this way, it is not always possible to accurately align the sensor with the polarization of the electromagnetic fields and an alternative alignment technique should be used instead.

- The investigator should position the meter so that it is parallel to the floor and to use a magnetic compass in order to align the measuring axis of the sensor with one of the cardinal points of the compass, e.g., North.

- Alternatively, or in situations when a compass is not

available, the sensor's measuring axis should be aligned with a main feature of the building. This may be the front or rear wall; if outdoors, a prominent landmark or feature can be used.

Measurements which are made using these methods of aligning the sensor may not always accurately represent the true intensity of the electromagnetism but the methods can be used to provide worthwhile data when it is not otherwise practical to align the sensor with the polarization of the field.

10.3 *Additional notes for single-axis sensors*

When several EMF meters are being used at the same time, the investigator must ensure that each meter is using the same method of alignment, e.g., to the electromagnetic field or to a compass point or location feature. If it is the latter, all of the devices must be using the same compass point or location feature. Each user should clearly indicate in their notes or records which method of alignment was being used when making their measurements.

When examining the EMF data, it is important that the investigator avoids making any comparisons between measurements which were obtained using different methods for aligning the sensor.

Single-axis meters will always require a greater degree of care to be taken by the investigator in order to obtain the most accurate and reliable measurements. The process of ensuring the accuracy of each measurement can sometimes be time consuming but if it is not properly undertaken the results are likely to be misleading and erroneous.

10.4 *Three-axis sensors*

Triaxial meters are capable of measuring the intensity of the field, without the user needing to align the sensor. This allows them to be conveniently placed when making extended measurements. When several meters are being used, ensure that they are aligned in a similar direction as this can improve the precision of the measurements that are being gathered. Three-axis devices have the same caveats as single-axis designs when they are being used hand-held. They are still be susceptible to movement, to other nearby devices and the proximity of the user's body.

10.5 *Finding the source*

The aim of the investigator should always be to locate the cause and the source of any detected electromagnetic field. It is rarely ever be the case that an investigator who is equipped with a frequency <u>and</u> amplitude measuring EMF meter will find it impossible to determine the cause and the source of any manmade or naturally occurring electromagnetic field that they encounter. However, those using simple, amplitude-only devices may find this to be much more difficult.

Investigators will already be aware of the need to turn off their mobile phones and radios in order to avoid their transmissions interfering with the EMF measurements. However, they often overlook many of the other devices they are likely to be using. Cameras, audio recorders, computers and even some torches (flashlights) are all known to be causes of interference and of erroneous measurements; this is also the case with mobile phones that have been placed into a flight-safe mode or radios that are not transmitting. A number of purpose-built ghost-hunting devices intentionally emit an electromagnetic field which can interfere with the investigator's measurements. Therefore, any device which the investigator is using that has the potential for interfering with the desired measurements should be switched off or removed to a safe distance whenever measurements of electromagnetic fields are being made.

! SAFETY WARNING !
Electricity Kills. The investigator must not attempt to interfere with electrical wiring that is not properly isolated from the electricity supply. If they suspect any type of electrical fault or failure, they MUST always consult a qualified electrician.

It is common for some investigators to presume that the most likely source of a detected electromagnetic field will be the location's electrical wiring or some electrical appliance, and in many instances, this will be the case. In these situations, simply locating the highest field intensity may sometimes be sufficient to allow the investigator to determine the source. Places where electrical connections are being made are all potential sources of interference and oftentimes, the source will be traced to a junction box or fuse board. The wiring itself is less likely to be the cause as it is normally well insulated and shielded. Nevertheless, the investigator is advised to always examine any wires which are visible, checking for breakages or old and worn insulation which can result in increased electromagnetic emissions. Turning off the power, either to that portion of the wiring that is suspected or to the entire location, may help to the investigator to locate a suspected cause within the electricity supply.

Electric appliances are a frequent cause of observed electromagnetic fields. An intermittent change in the intensity of the field can often be traced to an appliance, such as a refrigerator or thermostatically controlled heater switching on or off. In these cases, noting the times and the duration of the events can often provide the investigator with important clues that will assist them to locate these intermittent sources. It is also worthwhile consulting the building's owner or operator to find out if or when any intermittently switched appliances and devices are being used.

Observing the field's characteristics may be helpful when the source is due to appliances which are located in nearby buildings or external electrical installations which may be pole mounted or buried beneath the ground. A useful clue, which can sometimes indicate damaged or worn electricity supply apparatus, is to note any changes which occur during periods of wet weather or immediately afterwards. During wet and damp weather, faulty installations may cause increased levels of electromagnetism to be seen; occasionally, it is also possible to hear a buzz or hum associated with this type of fault. Underground faults are harder to detect and to demonstrate, but systematic measurements of the intensity of the field at regularly spaced intervals above the ground may reveal their position.

There may be occasions when the electromagnetic field will still be present, even after the investigator has turned off the electricity supply or at locations which have no power. The electrical wiring itself, regardless of whether the power is on or off, can sometimes act as an antenna, capable of re-radiating the electromagnetic field from a radio transmitter. This is especially the case, in any instance where the electromagnetic field appears to be coming from the electrical wiring after the power has been turned off. These re-radiated radio transmissions are also a strong candidate for other electromagnetic fields which seem to have no apparent cause but which appear to emanate from inside of the building or somewhere close-by. Other common sources of these secondary electromagnetic fields can be metalwork and structural elements of the building, metal water pipes and in some rare instances, even the internal wiring of some appliances. All of these can act as antennae, and may have an electromagnetic field surrounding them, the origin of which, i.e., the radio transmitter, may lie a considerable distance from the investigation site.

In addition to re-radiated radio transmissions, direct radio transmissions are also often detectable and measurable using an ordinary EMF meter. Sources include VHF and UHF radio transmitters, located within a few miles of the investigation site; the signal may also originate from a medium or longwave transmitter situated hundreds of miles or more distant. Signals from these more distant sources can often be influenced by the prevailing atmospheric conditions which may cause the observed electromagnetic field strength to vary considerably. Unless the investigator is using an EMF meter that is able to show the frequency of the electromagnetic field, it is extremely difficult for them to say with any degree of confidence that a radio transmitter is the cause of the observed electromagnetic field. However, by systematically observing the field's strength, noting how it rises or falls and measuring the strength of the field in different areas of the site it is sometimes possible to discern clues that may suggest the source. For example, public broadcast FM radio stations (e.g., BBC Radio 1) are usually indicated by a constant and unchanging field strength. Public broadcast AM radio stations (e.g., BBC World Service) are typically indicated by an electromagnetic field that is also continuous but which has variations in the strength; these variations may occur over several minutes, slowly fading up and down, or they may be small, more rapid fluctuations which can be observed using a sensitive EMF meter. Intermittent or randomly occurring electromagnetic fields, often only lasting a few seconds or rarely a few minutes, can frequently be linked with the operation of an occasional transmitter such is as used for aeronautical radio or by the emergency services and public utilities including taxis, cellular phone masts and radio data links.

10.6 *Surveying the location*

In some circumstances, it may be desirable to carry out a complete survey of the electromagnetic fields at an investigation site. If this is required, then it is recommended to use a three-axis meter whenever possible. However, if only a single-axis meter is available then the investigator should first align the meter, using one of the recommended methods described earlier in this chapter (**see Secs. 10.1 & 10.2**).

A single measuring point will rarely provide the investigator with a true representation of the electromagnetic fields throughout an entire room or space. However, a single measurement taken in the middle of the room (horizontally and vertically) may occasionally be used to gain an indication about the levels of ambient electromagnetism that exists therein. If additional measurements are to be made in other rooms or parts of the location, it is important that the sensor is aligned in the same way prior to each measurement. Aligning the sensor with a compass point or prominent feature of the location will usually suffice for these types of measurement.

To undertake a more complete sample of the electromagnetic fields within a room or space, the investigator should make a series of simultaneous measurements that are spaced evenly throughout the room. This process can only be carried out effectively by using several EMF meters. In urgent circumstances, it is possible to make a series of measurements throughout a room using only one EMF meter, however this is a time-consuming process that may not accurately account for any variations that occur during the time taken to complete the measurements. The importance of sensor alignment should not be overlooked.

The measurements should be made by dividing the space into one-metre boxes, horizontally and vertically and taking a single measurement in the centre of each box. The individual measurements can then be used to provide an average value for a single room or to highlight regions of electromagnetic variation within the location.

At larger investigation sites it may be advantageous to increase the separation between the individual measuring points.

10.7 *Baseline measurements*

The investigator may wish to make a continuous series of measurements as a point of reference for all other electromagnetic field measurements. Electromagnetic fields can change quickly and in order for the data to accurately reflect these changes, measurements need to be made several times per minute. Using a data-logging three-axis device is undoubtedly the best choice of device for obtaining this information. The EMF data-logger should be located in a suitable central position, away from any appliances or equipment that may interfere with the measurements. Measurements should commence at or before the start of the investigation session and continue throughout. (also **see Sec. 2.5**)

10.8 *Recording the measurements*

With the exception of data-logging models, the majority of EMF meters used by investigators require their measurements to be made and recorded manually. Irrespective of whether the EMF measurements are automated or taken manually, the data must indicate the time that every individual measurement was taken, together with the precise location where each was obtained and the measuring units that were used. It is also important that the investigator notes the make and model of each EMF meter being used (and its location/s), the orientation of the sensor (for single-axis meters) and which axes were being measured (for three-axis meters). This information provides important context and detail, allowing the data to be properly understood and is helpful for any subsequent investigations.

To assist manual measurements, a pre-prepared chart is recommended for each individual meter and measuring position. This simplifies the process of recording both the measurements and the contextual information. Records should be in a format that is readily understood and which allows the investigator to collate the information at a later time or date. In instances where it has been possible to determine the orientation or the source of an electromagnetic field, this may be indicated on a plan or map of the investigation site. It may also be helpful to indicate regions in which any unusual measurements have been discovered, where their source has not yet been determined.

10.9 *Using the EMF data*

In many respects, EMF data is similar to temperature data, i.e., it is a series of numeric values which the investigator can use to determine either the overall level of electromagnetism throughout the location or to assist them when searching for sources and causes of detected electromagnetic fields. With electromagnetic fields that have not yet had their source determined, it is worthwhile consulting the notes that were made during the investigation. These notes may contain information regarding the time and duration of the field and any observed variations in its intensity or orientation. This information may be helpful in understanding the nature or source of the unknown electromagnetic field (see **Sec. 10.5**). In some instances, their EMF measurements and other investigation records may suggest that a possible link exists between an observed electromagnetic field and reported paranormal experiences. However, such instances are excessively rare and difficult to demonstrate; only by carefully made measurements and thorough documentation may any potential link be highlighted and explored.

11 | Sound Recording

Unusual and unexpected sounds are amongst the most common phenomena that are reported by witnesses and also by those who are carrying out an investigation of a location.

Using equipment in order to record sound allows the investigator to determine if the reported sound was a real occurrence or if it may have been an auditory hallucination.

An examination of the recording can be used to discover more about the sound, for example how long did it last? What was its amplitude and frequency range? Did the recorded sound match the witness accounts?

Sound is produced by small variations in air pressure created by the motions of a vibrating surface acting upon the adjacent air. These small alterations in the air pressure, in turn, act upon the ear or the diaphragm in a microphone, allowing the sounds to be heard and recorded. Sound waves are also capable of travelling through other mediums including solids, liquids and gases. The speed at which the sound waves move is affected by the density of the medium through which it passes; for example, the speed of sound in air is about 343 metres / second but this can vary slightly depending upon the temperature and density of the air.

When describing the characteristics of sound, some of the terminology, e.g., frequency and amplitude, is the same as that which is used when describing electromagnetism and this can on occasions cause some people to become confused between the two. Sound recording is also confused with electronic voice phenomena (EVP) experiments. EVP experimenters also use sound recording equipment but the objectives of their experiments differ from those of ordinary sound recording. Please refer to the section on EVP for specific information (see **Sec.13**).

11.1 *Choosing a sound recorder*

There are two methods for recording sound; analogue and digital. Both methods are used by investigators, although digital recording has become the predominant means for recording sound during an investigation. Regardless of the type of recorder that is used, in order to derive the most useful information from any recording, the investigator should always try to obtain the best quality recording that is possible.

Analogue recorders store a direct reproduction of the electrical signal that is produced by the microphone. The signal from the microphone must then be amplified to a sufficient level for it to be recorded. The amplification process creates unwanted electrical interference which is reproduced on the recording as noise in the form of hiss. This is exacerbated by additional noise and distortions caused by the electro-mechanical components within the recorder and the tape. With each successive analogue copy that is made, the level of unwanted noise and distortion increases and the original sound becomes progressively more obscured. Recording durations are limited by the type of tape or cassette that is being used. Despite these drawbacks, high quality analogue recordings may reproduce a more complete representation of the original sound than some digital formats.

Digital recorders sample the microphone's electrical signal many thousands of times every second. These samples are then converted into a digital representation of the original signal which is then recorded in the same way as any other computer file. Digital recordings are less prone to electro-mechanical noise and distortion. Some file formats, such as the commonly used MP3, may restrict the range of frequencies and reduce the quality of the recording. Successive digital copies are not degraded.

Digital recording offers several significant advantages to the investigator; digital recorders have few, if any, moving parts meaning that they are generally more rugged and reliable than analogue tape recorders. The recording times can be many times longer than with tape, limited only by the amount of memory that is available. Recordings are easier to access and examine afterwards using a computer.

When selecting a sound recorder, the investigator should consider the intended use and if the model adequately meets those requirements. Is it for recording location sounds or recording witness interviews, or both? A recorder which allows the user to connect one or more external microphones offers a greater degree of flexibility and usability than those which have only a built-in microphone. Recorders which can use both batteries and an external power supply can extend the duration of the available recording time and permit the recorder to be used in a greater range of situations.

Devices with non-removeable memory have a finite limit to their recording duration, after which the memory must be cleared before further recordings can be made. Some non-removable memory recorders have a default loop-recording option which will continuously over-write earlier recordings unless this option is turned off. Recorders that use a removeable memory need only to have the memory card changed at appropriate intervals.

Options for selecting the recording quality are desirable. Being able to change the sampling rate and bit depth and to select a non-compressed file format (digital) or to increase the tape speed (analogue) will assist the investigator to get the best audio quality.

Useability is also an important consideration. Recorders that have complicated controls, requiring multiple buttons presses and menu selections, are likely to result in the recorder being incorrectly set-up, leading to poor quality or even missed recordings. Some recorders have additional options including special effects, which are unlikely to ever be needed by investigators. Before purchasing, check the specifications carefully and read the product reviews. It can often be more helpful to read reviews and comments posted on sites and forums that are aimed at non-paranormal users such as musicians and sound recording engineers.

11.2 *Getting the best recording quality*

Options for adjusting the quality of the recordings will vary from recorder to recorder; users should always consult the instruction manual for their particular device.

Regardless of whether the recorder is analogue or digital, it is recommended that the user turns off any noise reduction or sound enhancing controls, for example: Equalization, Dolby© noise reduction, compressor, limiter, bass or treble boost. Sound effects such as echo, reverb or those which mimic different rooms and spaces, e.g., large hall, studio etc. should also be turned off. Using any of these will permanently alter the way in which the sound is recorded.

Another common option provided is a wind-cut filter (sometimes called lo-cut or bass-cut). This may sometimes be helpful when recording out of doors where excessive wind noise can obscure the audio recording but otherwise it should be turned off.

Voice activated recording options should be turned off. If it is used, important preceding information may not be recorded and some quieter sounds may not be recorded at all. This may limit the context of the sound recording or reduce the investigator's ability to make a proper assessment of the recording.

11.2.1 *Analogue recording*

Always use a good quality type I or type II cassette tape. If the recorder has a tape type selector switch, this should be set for the type of tape that is being used.

Choose the highest possible tape speed, e.g., the speed at which the tape passes the recording head. This option may be indicated in either inches or centimetres per second or it may be abbreviated to indicate the recording quality, e.g., HQ (High Quality), SP (Standard Play), and LP (Long Play). Higher tape speeds reduce the amount of noise (hiss) on the recording but also reduce the duration of the available recording time. Periodically, clean the recording head and tape transport mechanism following the manufacturer's instructions. If these are not available, then using isopropyl alcohol on a cotton bud is suggested.

11.2.2 *Digital recording*

Choose a good quality memory card of sufficient capacity to allow a high sample rate and a reasonable recording time. As a guide, a 32Gb memory card will allow a recording time of approximately six or seven hours to be made at the higher quality settings.

Wherever possible use an uncompressed audio format, for example, .wav or .btw file. Compressed file formats, for example, .mp3 or .AAC should be avoided wherever possible as file compression method removes audio data which cannot be restored.

For most investigation situations, selecting a sample rate of 44.1 kbps or 48 kbps at 16- or 24-bit depth, will provide recordings of sufficient quality. Using an uncompressed sample rate of either 96kbps or 192kbps at 24- or 32-bit depths can sometimes reveal additional information but doing so may lead to aliasing and the introduction of false frequency data. Higher sampling rates also increase the file size and the amount of memory that is required.

11.2.3 *Audio input level*

Many recorders provide some means for controlling the level of the sound that is being recorded. It may be labelled in various ways; e.g., microphone gain, audio level or input volume. Some recorders have pre-set input levels labelled with typical recording situations, e.g., quiet, noisy, lecture, concert. Regardless of how it is labelled, the audio input level regulates the amount of amplification that is applied to the audio input (microphone) signal. It may be tempting to set this control to its maximum but this should be avoided, even in the quietest of locations. Setting the input level control to its highest value is likely to introduce excessive electronic noise from the amplifier circuitry. As a guide, input levels of around 40-60% are normally suitable for making good quality recordings in situations in which people are speaking normally, this may be increased to around 50-70% in quiet locations and in extremely quiet locations an input of 70-80% will almost always suffice.

The use of automatic level control (ALC) or automatic recording gain control (AGC) options should be avoided. Whenever possible, ALC or AGC controls should either be turned off, or turned to their lowest setting. The use of ALC or AGC can cause excessive fluctuations in the level of the recorded audio as the automatic control responds to changes in the ambient sound level.

11.3 *Make a test recording*

Once the recording equipment has been set up in its intended operating position it is recommended that a test recording is made. This can then be listened to and any necessary adjustments made. Making a test recording is especially important when the investigator intends to record an interview. After the equipment is set up and the participants are settled, a short test recording allows final adjustments to be made to the input levels and microphone positions before the interview commences. It is perfectly acceptable to indicate to the interviewee how far from the microphone they should be.

When listening to a test recording, it is recommended to always use a pair of closed back over-ear headphones, similar to those used by sound recording engineers. Using the built-in speaker or inexpensive earbuds is unlikely to provide the user with an accurate representation of the audio quality and may fail to reveal other problems with the recording.

The test recording also serves to ensure that the recorder and the microphone are operating correctly.

11.4 *Common recording problems*

It is unfortunately commonplace for investigators to present evidential recordings in which the recorded sound is muffled or almost indiscernible. Sometimes, the cause of the poor quality lies in the investigator's choice of equipment or the manner in which it was operated. The inexpensive MP3 recorders which are often promoted and sold for use by investigators are rarely suitable for even the most rudimentary of recording tasks. Microphones too may be unsuitable for their intended use, or of poor quality.

Oftentimes, the cause of the poor recording quality can be quickly rectified by the user making a few additional checks beforehand or making some simple changes to the way in which they are using the equipment.

11.5 *Extraneous noises*

Unwanted sounds and noises are often heard on some recordings and may sometimes result in the investigator thinking that they are anomalous. Often these extraneous sounds are caused by handling noise when the recorder is being hand-held. Unwanted sounds can be picked up through the body of the recorder. Both types of noise can be especially troublesome with recorders that use a built-in microphone (see **Sec. 12.2**).

Handling noise can often be cured by simply putting the recorder down, although in some instances this may not be practical. Some recorders have an attachment point, to allow the device to be mounted onto a camera or tripod. This can also be used to attach a small tripod which can be used as a handle. Holding the recorder in this way often greatly reduces handling noise and in many instances is also a more comfortable and convenient method of holding the device. The method may be further improved by using one of the recorder suspension mounts that are available; these are designed to use the same camera tripod attachment point and are an effective means of isolating the recorder from any handling sounds. If the recorder lacks any means of attaching it to a tripod / handle then as a last resort, holding the device firmly, away from the built-in microphone and minimising movements of the hand or the recorder will often reduce handling noise to an acceptable level.

Noises picked up through the recorder's body can be reduced in a similar way. Using a suspension mount to attach the recorder to a tripod (full size or table-top) is often the most effective method for preventing this cause of unwanted noise, but it may not always be the most practical solution. In situations when the recorder needs to be quickly set-up, placing it onto a soft surface, e.g., a cushion or folded cloth, is preferable to placing it onto a hard table-top or floor. Some investigators carry a small bath sponge with them, placing the recorder on the sponge is a simple but effective method for reducing sounds picked up via the recorder's body.

11.6 *Audio distortion*

Recordings that are distorted may often cause significant problems for the investigator, in some instances they can result in the entire recording becoming unusable or result in wasted time trying to discern what has been recorded. In many cases, the cause of the problem can be easily found and rectified. Often, it is simply a control that is incorrectly set e.g., the input level may be turned too high. Sometimes, a power cord or the plug on an external microphone may not be properly connected or may be dirty and preventing a proper connection being made. Batteries which are rundown or nearly so, can be a common cause for a distorted recording. Fresh batteries should be used for each recording session and spares carried. If the recorder uses an external power supply, this should be of the correct voltage and also be capable of delivering sufficient power.

Audio distortion may indicate a problem with the microphone. Wet or damp conditions and condensation can adversely affect the operation of many microphones. Some microphones require power in order to operate; this may be supplied by an internal battery or from the recorder by means of the microphone cable (phantom power). If the power supply to the microphone is insufficient then audio distortion is likely to occur. Microphone cables and connecting plugs are another common source of distorted recordings; they are prone to wear and damage and should be periodically checked. Using an inappropriate cover in order to protect the microphone can cause significant audio distortion, for example, placing the microphone inside a plastic bag or into a pocket. In rare instances, the distortion may indicate that the microphone is faulty and needing to be replaced.

Poor quality or distorted audio can sometimes indicate that a poor-quality tape or memory card has been used. There is a temptation to purchase cassette tapes or memory cards that are being offered at a lower price. Sometimes, these are reputable products and represent a genuine cost saving. Unfortunately, there are also many copies and counterfeits of much lower quality. Cassette tapes are still available in some supermarkets and online but it is worthwhile checking the packaging as some have a manufacturing date which can be checked. Avoid old stock that may have been incorrectly stored and be aware that cassette tapes can also be inferior quality counterfeits.

One final, albeit rare problem that sometimes occurs with recordings is caused by poor storage of the recordings either immediately after use or later. Some of the devices that are used by investigators contain powerful magnets. If these are placed in close proximity to a cassette tape and even some memory cards it can result in partial or complete disruption of the recording that they contain. This may even occur when the tape or the card is inside the recorder. Keep any devices that contain magnets as far away as is practical from any type of recording media. This applies not only when they are packed into the investigation kit bag but also afterwards when they may be stored or archived.

11.7 *Sound level measurement*

Sound level meters are used by some investigators. These devices measure the level of sound that is present. They are normally used for determining safe levels of environmental sound in order to safeguard hearing or for monitoring noise pollution. They are also used by sound engineers to set up and balance audio systems. There seems little purpose in the investigator routinely measuring sound levels. If a sound does require its level to be accurately assessed this can often be done using the recording and suitable provisioned sound analysis software. Sound level meters are inexpensive, and they can occasionally be useful in some particular applications, including determining the likely presence of infrasound. However, in the majority of investigations, measuring the amplitude of the sound is of little value and the time may be better spent on other parts of the investigation.

11.8 *Inaudible sounds*

Investigators have become interested in sounds that are ordinarily inaudible to the human ear; this may be due to either the frequency or to the amplitude of the sound waves. Sound waves which lie outside of the normal human frequency range of hearing are often referred to as infrasound (very low frequencies) and ultrasound (very high frequencies).

11.8.1 *Infrasound*

This is normally considered to be any sound whose frequency is below 20Hz. Infrasound can be naturally occurring or man-made, and the low frequency sound waves are able to travel very long distances from the source and are extremely difficult to block, meaning that Infrasound is present to some degree at almost every location. There are a number of studies which have linked exposure to infrasound and other low frequency sounds to reports of paranormal experiences. Therefore, it is natural that investigators would be interested in measuring low frequency sounds at investigation sites.

Whilst it is not technically difficult to detect the presence of low frequency sound, it cannot be recorded or its intensity accurately determined using ordinary sound recording and measuring equipment. Sound recording equipment, including microphones, recorders and computer sound cards are specifically designed to minimise the pick-up of low frequency sound as doing so would cause significant distortion (rumble) to the audible sound. Similarly, the majority of sound measuring equipment is designed to only respond and measure sounds that are within the normal human hearing range.

Fortunately, there is a simple technique that investigators may use which allows the presence of low frequency sounds to be indicated. The method only requires an ordinary sound level meter. In some instances, a smartphone sound meter App can also be used, however, the built-in microphone may limit its effectiveness. In order for this technique to work the sound meter (or App) must have both 'A' and 'C' measurement weighting options. If the meter has a 'Peak Hold' function, this should also be used.

- Set the meter to the A weighting option and measure the level of the ambient sound. Note the highest value observed or shown on the peak hold during a one-minute period.

- Repeat, this time using the C weighting option and again note the highest observed value.

If the value of the C weighted measurement is greater than the value of the A weighted measurement, this may indicate the presence of low frequency sound. The greater the difference between the C weighted value and the A weighted value, the greater becomes the likelihood that low frequency sound is present at the measuring location. If the value of C is significantly higher than the value of A, e.g., more than 10dBs, it is likely that an appreciable level of infrasound is present at the measuring location.

Note: The method only provides the investigator with an indication that low frequency sound is present. It cannot be used to obtain a measured value for the low frequency sound. If the difference between the two weighted values is less than 3dBs then no determination should be made, as this difference lies within the operating tolerances of the sound measuring equipment.

Infrasound, like all types of sound, can be transient and its level can change quickly. Longer measuring periods may be useful in order to account for these variances in sound level.

The presence of infrasound can also be inferred by using a vibration measuring device. Some devices have the facility to indicate the frequency of the vibrations. Some of these vibrations may be the result of sound waves causing vibrations at the same low frequency in the structure or material being tested. Once again, this cannot provide an accurate measurement of the sound level but it can offer the investigator a further means for determining if infrasound or low frequency sounds are present.

11.8.2 *Ultrasound*

This is normally considered to be any sound whose frequency is above 20kHz. Ultrasound can occur naturally or it can be man-made. Ultrasound waves are only able to travel for short distances and are readily blocked or attenuated. The source of the ultrasound is therefore likely to always lie in close proximity to the point at which it is being detected.

Little attention has yet been given by investigators to these very high frequency inaudible sounds but they are known to cause some physiological disruption to those who are exposed to these sound frequencies, and ultrasound is used in several devices for crowd control. Ultrasound is also not easy to accurately measure or record using conventional sound equipment which is not designed to respond to these high frequencies. Some sound meters (and Apps) are able to measure sound frequencies above 20kHz but few are able to reach a significant way into the ultrasound region. Some vibration measuring devices are capable of measuring physical vibrations at frequencies in the ultrasonic region. However, there is generally insufficient energy for the sound waves to cause physical vibrations in many structures so this method is likely to prove unsuccessful. Moreover, at extremely high frequencies, e.g., those in excess of 35kHz, the soundwaves will travel barely a few metres before they become significantly attenuated by the air.

Due to the complexity of measuring or even detecting ultrasound and a lack of any significant data to suggest that measuring it might be worthwhile, investigators are advised to waste little time undertaking any measurements of these frequencies.

11.8.3 *Other inaudible sounds*

It is not just the frequency of the sound that determines its audibility; the amplitude or volume of the sound is also a determining factor in how it is heard and perceived. Sounds that are ordinarily too quiet to be heard by the ear may still be perceived by the brain. This is especially the case with sounds that lie very close to the threshold of hearing; sometimes, these threshold sounds may still be capable of unconsciously influencing the individual. They may report these occurrences as unusual, for example: "I thought I could hear something, but as hard as I listened, everything was quiet".

Human hearing limits vary widely from person to person and the ability to hear sound diminishes with age. Disease and illness can also adversely affect the ability of an individual to hear sound. Sound recorders do not have the same variations in what they can 'hear'. The volume of the ambient sounds which they are able to record is set by the technical characteristics of the recorder and the microphone. Therefore, it is commonplace for a sound recording to contain sounds which the investigator did not hear, but were present at the time that the recording was being made. Sometimes, these ordinary sounds are mistaken or interpreted as being evidence of electronic voice phenomena (EVP).

Investigators who use a spectrum analyser to examine their sound recordings may often discover that there is a significant amount of sound contained in their recordings that is not being heard. Some of this may be electronic and mechanical noise but a great deal is sound that is simply too quiet to be heard. Sometimes it is possible to amplify these sounds in order to make them audible but this method will also amplify the unwanted noise. Nevertheless, in some situations, the investigator may find it is helpful to apply a small controlled amount of amplification when listening to their recordings.

12 | Microphones

Every recording system shares the necessity of needing a microphone in order to be able to translate the sound into a form that can be recorded. The importance of the microphone is often overlooked by investigators. The choice of microphone and the way in which it is used will significantly affect the quality of recordings that are made, regardless of the recorder. Different situations will often need a different type of microphone. Investigators are advised to consider acquiring several different microphones to suit different situations and locations.

12.1 *Dynamic and condenser microphones*

All microphones are analogue devices. They produce an electrical signal which is directly representative of, and proportional to, the soundwaves reaching the device. There are essentially two types of microphone; dynamic and condenser, although there are many variations and designs within each type.

Dynamic microphones have a thin non-conductive diaphragm, to which is attached a coil of fine wire. This in turn is surrounded by a non-moving permanent magnet. Movement of the diaphragm in response to sound waves causes the coil to move past the magnet and this generates a signal voltage within the coil. The very small signal voltage must be amplified, in order for it to be usable. Dynamic microphones require no power in order to operate and the design is normally physically robust. They are typically less sensitive to quieter sounds and are not generally suitable for applications such as directional sound gathering, or where a small form factor is required, such as a lapel microphone.

Condenser microphones also use a diaphragm; this is made to be electrically conductive and forms part of an electrical circuit in which the output voltage changes in proportion to changes in the sound. Condenser microphones always require some form of power in order to operate and the more delicate components can be adversely affected by rough handling, humidity or moisture. These microphones are generally more sensitive to quiet sounds and require less signal amplification, but poor designs can introduce unwanted electrical noise. Condenser microphones are suitable for use in many applications and are the most common type of microphone that is likely to be encountered.

12.2 *Built-in and plug-in microphones*

Many recorders include a built-in microphone and in models which lack any means to connect an external microphone, this is the only microphone option that is available. Using a built-in microphone can be convenient, allowing the investigator to make sound recordings without needing to also set up an additional microphone. Built-in microphones are of the condenser type and draw their power directly from the recorder.

Built-in microphones can be highly variable in their quality; cheaper recorders often have a small (1/8th inch) microphone capsule with a restricted frequency range and poor sound reproduction. Exceptions do exist, but a helpful method for discerning the likely quality of a built-in microphone is to look at the microphone aperture on the device. If it is simply a small hole (barely bigger than a pin-hole) then it will be a small capsule microphone. These are unsuitable for location sound recording and are better suited for recording voice memos or perhaps an occasional witness interview.

Some of the latest generation equipment is capable of providing high quality recordings using only the built-in microphone, but others can be disappointing. In some situations, the built-in microphones will be perfectly adequate; the investigator is advised to carry out their own test recordings and experiments beforehand.

There are a growing number of recorders which use one (or sometimes two) high quality microphones, with a larger diameter capsule (¼ or ½ inch). These are intended for use by musicians and other professional users who require high quality sound reproduction and are therefore a much better option for investigators to consider. Some of these recorders also allow the user to adjust the directionality and sensitivity of the built-in microphone to suit different recording applications.

A compromise solution may be to use one of the plug-in large capsule microphones that are increasingly available for smartphone and tablet recorders. These mount directly onto the device and use the USB or other proprietary input connection. These microphones offer much better quality than the built-in microphone and in some instances are the same type of microphones that are used by recorders which are intended for professional use.

A significant drawback with many built-in and plug-on microphones can be acoustic pick-up through the recorder's body. If the microphone is not properly physically isolated from the body of the recorder even slight vibrations and handling sounds can be picked up. These extraneous sounds can sometimes be unexpectedly loud, causing the recording to become unusable. In some instances, the handling noises can be mistaken for unusual or anomalous sounds. Using a recorder with a built-in microphone often requires that a compromise must be made when positioning the device; the best position for the microphone may not always be the easiest location for accessing and operating the recorder.

Choosing a recorder which lets the user connect one or more external microphones is normally a better option. Different recording situations and varied recording locations often require different microphones to be necessary, in order to obtain the best sound quality. Using an external microphone allows the investigator to select the most suitable microphone for any particular location and recording situation.

12.3 *Microphone pick-up patterns*

Microphones rarely pick-up the sound uniformly; most have some form of directionality. Those with only a small degree of directionality are referred to as being omni-directional, other designs may be highly directional. Microphone models are often optimised for specific applications, e.g., performance, studio, speech etc. When selecting a microphone, the pick-up pattern of the microphone should be matched as closely as possible with the intended use.

12.3.1 *Omni-directional microphones*

As the name indicates, omni-directional microphones have a very low degree of directionality and will respond to sounds arriving from any direction. Therefore, they are often the best choice for general recording situations, such as the ambient sounds within a room or a group of people sitting around a table. Wherever possible, this type of microphone should be positioned centrally and equidistant from the sound sources. An omni-directional microphone is much less effective when it is placed close to a floor or wall as it can pick up reflected sounds from the adjacent surfaces, causing distortion and reverberation on the recording.

12.3.2 *Directional microphones – cardioid microphones*

This design has a sensitivity that is greater in one direction and correspondingly less in the opposite direction. The sound pick-up pattern resembles a heart shape; hence the alternative name. The direction in which the microphone is most sensitive is normally indicated on the microphone body; this will normally be along the primary axis of the microphone. Directional microphones are also a good choice in many recording situations, especially those where it is difficult to position a microphone centrally; instead, it can be aimed towards the speaker or other intended sound source. Directional microphones are also helpful in situations where the investigator wishes to reduce the amount of sound being picked up from an unwanted source.

12.3.3 *Highly directional microphones – shotgun microphones*

The name is derived from the design which resembles a gun barrel. This type of microphone is highly directional and is most useful in situations where the investigator needs to record the sounds from a specific direction whilst also minimising the sounds coming from other directions. The design is also helpful when the investigator wishes to record within a long and narrow space such as a corridor as it can be highly effective at reducing unwanted sound reverberations that may interfere with the quality of the recording.

12.4 *Frequency range of the microphone*

The frequency range of a microphone is an important consideration and should not be overlooked by investigators when they are choosing which microphone to use. The frequency range of the microphone should closely match that of the chosen audio recorder; there is no advantage in using a microphone that can pick up sounds that the recorder cannot reproduce. However, it is better to select a microphone with a frequency range that slightly exceeds that of the recorder rather than one which is less.

Manufacturers will normally include an indication of the operating frequency range of the microphone in its specifications. However, this information should be considered as being only a guide; the actual frequency response may be different due to the placement of the microphone and the accuracy of the manufacturer's claims. Inexpensive generic microphones often just state a frequency range of twenty Hertz (20Hz) to twenty kilo Hertz (20kHz) which equates to the normal human range of human hearing.

Microphones intended for studio or broadcast applications are more costly but they are capable of producing much higher quality sound; moreover, the frequency specifications are likely to be more accurate. Some designs which do have a wide frequency range may be optimised to be more sensitive to a particular range of frequencies such as the human voice and although they are still capable of reproducing audio at other frequencies, their response may be significantly poorer outside the optimal range.

12.5 *Microphone design*

Normally the design of a microphone will be governed by its intended use, although occasionally, the design will owe more to aesthetics or to marketing than to function. Some of designs, such as the boundary microphone and the lavaliere microphone, can provide the investigator with a worthwhile advantage, whilst other designs may be less useful.

Boundary microphones, are omni directional condenser microphones that are designed to be placed on or very close to a large flat surface e.g., a table-top, floor or wall. They are primarily intended for use in situations where there are a number of widely separated speakers, such as at conferences, or when recording the sound in large spaces. The design can also be useful in situations where there may be a lot of reverberation. The frequency range is governed not only by the microphone capsule but to a great extent by the size and type of surface it is placed upon.

Lavaliere microphones, more commonly called lapel microphones, are also condenser microphones that are designed to be used by an individual speaker. They are normally attached directly onto the clothing of the speaker and aimed towards their mouth. Lavaliere microphones use a small capsule with a cardioid pick-up pattern and have a frequency response which is optimised for the human voice.

Parabolic microphones use a parabolic dish or reflector which allows them to be highly directional. This design is most often used for nature recording and in surveillance sound recording applications. The size of the dish affects the frequency response of the microphone and also the accuracy with which wanted sounds can be picked and unwanted sounds are rejected. Parabolic microphones are unwieldy and in the majority of investigation situations they are unlikely to provide any significant advantage over a shotgun microphone.

The popularity of podcasting has led to the introduction of a number of high-quality microphones that have a USB computer connection instead of a conventional microphone plug. Some investigators may prefer to use a laptop, tablet computer or even a smartphone as their primary sound recorder and using one of these USB microphones will provide a significant improvement over the built-in microphone that is fitted in these devices. This method of connecting the microphone is convenient and does away with the need for additional audio interfaces and cables. USB connected microphones cannot be connected to conventional sound recorder inputs, although a small number of microphones are available which offer both methods of connection and also, some recorders allow both types of connection to be made.

12.6 *Microphones to avoid*

There are also several small parabolic microphones which are sometimes sold as ghost hunting tools. In reality, these have a highly amplified small capsule microphone that is surrounded by an almost useless plastic dish. Using one of these will certainly make the sounds appear louder, but invariably this will be due to the level of amplification that is used, often at the expense of the quality of the sound that is reproduced. In almost every case, the investigator will find that the fidelity of their recording will be improved by using a good quality shotgun microphone. Caution should also be extended to other microphones which provide built-in amplification. Some of these are also advertised as ghost hunting devices, claiming to let the user hear or record sounds that are too quiet to be otherwise heard. Using one of these highly amplified microphones is likely to result in a distorted, noisy recording with a limited frequency range that is of little value to the investigator.

Investigators should be cautious when considering any low-cost unbranded microphone. These are more likely to contain substandard components and often have an uncertain frequency response and poor sensitivity, regardless of whatever claims the maker or the seller may make.

12.7 *Positioning and placement of the microphone*

It is common to see investigators placing the microphone down onto the floor, table or chair prior to making a recording. Unless this is a boundary microphone, doing so will invariably reduce the quality of the reproduced sound due to the proximity of the surface and vibrations that are passed through the microphone's body. It is strongly recommended that a suitable microphone stand, preferably one that has a shock absorbing mount, is used to minimise any vibration and other effects caused by the proximity of the surface. If a suitable microphone stand is not available then a useful tip is to use a small bath sponge as a support. The sponge both raises the microphone above the surface and isolates it from some of the vibrations that would otherwise be picked up.

Omni-directional microphones work best when they are placed centrally within the area to be recorded. If this includes a group of speakers, they should all be equidistant from the microphone. With omni-directional microphones, the orientation of the capsule is also an important factor to consider; some designs work best when they are placed vertically, whilst others work best with the microphone horizontal. If in doubt, placing the microphone at a 45° angle is a reasonable compromise.

Directional microphones should be positioned towards the direction of the desired sounds or away from any unwanted sound sources. Cardioid designs generally have their greatest sound rejection towards the rear of the microphone, whereas shotgun microphones are better at rejecting any unwanted sounds coming from the sides. With some cardioid models it may not be immediately apparent how the capsule is orientated, although most makers do mark this on the body or indicate this in the specifications. Shotgun designs should always be orientated so that the long axis (gun barrel) of the microphone is aimed toward the wanted sound source or at right angles to an unwanted sound. Designs do vary and users should always take some time to experiment and familiarise themselves beforehand. Directional microphones often perform better when they are placed a few feet out from the corner of a room, aimed towards its centre. If they are to be used in a long corridor, aim the microphone directly along the axis of the corridor with the microphone positioned a few feet from one end.

Lavaliere microphones should be placed on or close to the lapel. Normally the microphone is aimed toward the speaker's mouth but it is common for broadcasters to aim their lavaliere microphones away from the speaker's mouth in order to minimise breathing and popping sounds from occurring. Lavaliere microphones are sometimes prone to extraneous sounds, produced when they rub against clothing, zip fasteners and jewellery or of having their sound muffled by collars and clothing. To minimise these problems, always carry out a test recording beforehand; this should be done whilst the speaker carries out any movements or actions they will be doing during the recording, e.g., walking or indicating with their arms etc.

Boundary microphones should always be placed so that they are on or in very close proximity to a large, flat surface. They should be centrally located and work best when the surface they are upon is a hard non sound absorbing material. Tables and solid floors can be used but caution is needed as the microphone may also pick up extraneous sounds from people using other devices that are on the table or caused by people leaning on the table or walking around on the floor.

12.8 *Microphone accessories and care*

Choosing a good quality microphone is only part of ensuring that the recorded sound is of the highest possible quality. As has already been indicated, the placement and support for the microphone is a significant factor in ensuring the quality of the sound. There are innumerable microphone stands available, at a range of prices. The investigator is unlikely to require costly studio grade mounting systems but neither should they mount their microphone on something that is prone to picking up vibration and is barely able to hold the microphone in the desired position. Stands may be small table top designs or they may be a conventional floor standing type. Both are a good investment and allow the investigator to have a greater range of options for placing and supporting their microphones. A range of adaptors are also available that allow a microphone to be attached to a camera tripod.

Some microphones come supplied with a means for attaching the microphone to a stand; these are often in the form of a plastic moulding. These basic attachments rarely offer any form of vibration absorption. It is better to locate an accessory vibration damping microphone mount which will significantly reduce extraneous noises being picked up through the microphone's body.

Foam or fur wind shields are a good investment and should always be used in outdoor recording situations to minimise unwanted wind noise. Indoors, they may also be helpful, especially when the microphone is close to a speaker's mouth, in order to reduce the popping and sibilant distortions that can occur in these situations. For normal indoor ambient sound recording, they should be removed; doing so will increase the fidelity of the microphone slightly.

Cables, connectors and plugs are often overlooked but are important parts of the recording system. Microphone cables should be good quality shielded designs to minimise the picking up of electrical interference and other electromagnetic interference. Periodically the cable should be checked for broken or worn insulation or damaged connector plugs.

Microphones contain delicate components which may be damaged by rough handling or poor storage. Condensation is a particular problem for condenser microphones and can cause distorted sound and crackling sounds on the recordings. When not in use, the microphone should be stored in a cool, dry place and protected by a bag or case to prevent physical damage.

Some condenser microphones draw their power directly from the recorder via the microphone cable; other models, use an internal battery. Occasionally, the microphone can be powered using either method. If batteries are fitted, these can often last for hundreds of hours and in some designs, there is no option to turn the microphone off; they are powered the entire time the battery is fitted. This can result in the user forgetting to change the battery; often this just means that the microphone ceases to work, but it can lead to battery corrosion if the battery is left unchecked and the corrosive chemicals inside leak out. Microphones should be checked regularly and their battery inspected. If the microphone is unlikely to be used for some time, it is recommended that the battery be removed.

12.9 *Additional notes for microphone use*

It may be helpful to speak to a local community radio station about the types of microphone that they are using as their requirements will not be very different to those of investigators; radio stations also need to record location sounds and interviews. Many of these community stations operate with a restricted budget and will probably have already sought out the best quality affordable microphones that are available. It is also worthwhile visiting a local musician's store; most will allow you to bring your own recorder to try out with a range of microphones in order to find the most suitable and compatible models.

13 | Electronic Voice Phenomenon – EVP

Electronic voice phenomenon – EVP, originally referred to the appearance of voices and other speech-like utterances on audio recordings without the operator hearing the sounds when the recording was taking place. The voices are only apparent when the recording is played back and sometimes seem to respond to questions that are asked aloud by the operator. More recently, the term is also used to describe voices produced by means of an electronic device that incorporates a loudspeaker. This method is intended to let the operator hear any responses to their questions in real-time, with no need for them to wait for the recording to be played back. Both methods are employed by investigators at haunted locations although the latter method has become the most popular. There are numerous devices and software Apps which have been developed to facilitate investigators who wish to conduct their own experiments. The first real-time EVP devices were developed from radios that had been modified to cause them to scan across the frequencies without locking on to any particular station or broadcast.

Instrumental trans communication – ITC, is also occasionally used to describe electronic communications, although it is more usually applied to incidents of visual phenomena, such as the unexpected appearance of faces, human figures and text on television and computer screens. Video ITC is rarely used by location investigators.

It is widely presumed that the voices which appear are those of the deceased although there are others who consider the voices to be those of other discarnate spirits or aliens from other planets. Despite a lack of substantive evidence that the voices which are heard and recorded are truly anomalous in their origin, interest in undertaking EVP experiments remains high and EVP experiments are popular with many investigators.

EVP should not be confused with location sound recordings that may also be carried out during an investigation, although it is reported that EVP may sometimes occur in location sound recordings. EVP experimenters make extensive use of sound recording equipment and may find it helpful to also refer to the sections of these notes which deal with sound recording and microphones for additional guidance.

13.1 *Simple EVP recording methods*

Those who wish to conduct EVP experiments require very few items of equipment. Many of the early experimenters used only an ordinary sound recorder and microphone, with which they achieved many interesting results. The method they employed was simple, and it is still used by many of those who carry out EVP experiments as part of their investigations.

After commencing the recording, the investigator asks aloud a series of questions, pausing between each question to allow sufficient time for a response. Upon completion, the recording is played back and any responses are listened for.

The method does however, require care to be taken by the investigator, as it is possible to introduce extraneous sounds to the recording. These are easily caused by handling noises and the operation of switches and buttons, picked up through the body of the recorder. These extraneous sounds are more likely to occur in models that have the microphone built-in to the device. Holding the recorder should be avoided whenever possible but in situations where this is not practical, handling noises can be reduced by holding the device firmly, keeping the fingers as far from the microphone as possible.

Using an external microphone will greatly reduce incidents of handling noise but some microphones and microphones cables may be prone to unwanted handling noise and electrical interference. This is especially likely if the investigator is using a poor-quality microphone or an unshielded microphones cable. Using a microphone and cable which is designed for stage or studio use by musicians will significantly reduce handling noise and electrical interference from affecting the recording.

It is better to place the recorder down, but this may still result in knocks and vibrations being picked up through the recorder's body. These are much more likely to occur if the recorder is placed onto a hard surface. Wherever possible, the recorder should be placed onto a soft surface, such as a convenient chair cushion or several layers of folded cloth. Some investigators include a bath sponge in their investigation kit, which can be placed beneath the recorder in order to isolate it from a hard surface. If an external microphone is being used, this too, should be supported and isolated; ideally, by using a vibration absorbing microphone stand or even by using a second bath sponge. The microphone's capsule should be raised at least six inches above any hard surface in order to minimise reflected sounds being picked up by the microphone. To reduce cable noises and electrical interference, microphone cables and power cords should be kept well separated and touched as little as possible during the recording session.

Making several short recordings is preferable to a single extended session. Overly long recordings can be tedious for the listener. If the recording is overly noisy it can also be difficult or uncomfortable for them to listen to. It is recommended that the listener leaves a gap of several minutes between each individual recording, to allow them time to rest.

Prior to each new EVP recording session, it is important that the investigator reduces the likelihood of previous recordings bleeding through into later recordings. This is especially important for those who use analogue (tape) recorders. It is much less of a problem with digital recorders, although it can still occur. Investigators should always ensure that the cassettes they are using are properly erased. Ideally, this should be done using a dedicated tape erasing device. If this is not available, then it is recommended to make a blank recording by removing or turning off the microphone and disconnecting any other audio inputs. Cassettes should be used as few times as possible; ideally, they should be replaced before every new EVP session but this is often impractical. If cassettes are to be re-used, it is suggested that each individual tape should be replaced entirely after five sessions. This will minimise the inevitable degradation in audio quality that is caused by the tape moving through the mechanism and reduces bleed-through from previous recordings which becomes increasingly likely as the tape becomes worn. The same precautions are also advised for those who may be using one of the digital cassette tape formats, e.g., Digital Audio Tape (DAT).

The majority of digital recorders store their recordings onto either a magnetic hard disk or a solid state (fixed or removable) recording media. These can be re-used many hundreds of times without any discernible loss of audio quality. Digital recorders are not immune from previously erased recordings becoming mixed with later recordings and being mistaken for EVP. To minimise this, the investigator is advised to always re-format the recording media rather than simply erasing the previous recordings, this should be done prior to each new EVP session.

13.2 *Other EVP methods*

A number of EVP researchers have suggested that adding extra (audible) sound can assist the production of the recorded voices. This can be done using a loudspeaker located nearby, or by carrying out the EVP recordings in an inherently noisy location. Electronically produced white noise is used by some investigators whilst others prefer using everyday sounds such as running water, wind blowing through the trees or various genres of music. These additional sounds can be in the form of a recording or they may occur naturally at the location.

Many of the early EVP experimenters also used an ordinary radio as their primary means for hearing the voices. This method is much less used today, but investigators who use this method suggest tuning the radio to a particular frequency or station, or tuning in-between stations, so that only a continuous hiss can be heard from the loudspeaker.

Derived from the experiments conducted by EVP pioneer Konstantin Raudive, some investigators prefer to use a diode receiver instead of the microphone. Several devices and attachments are available which replicate Raudive's original diode receiver. Other devices, which are also described as 'Raudive diodes', have a variety of more recent innovations and modifications. These include, a built-in microphone which allows the operator to also record their questions and stereo devices containing two diode circuits. All of these diode attachments, including Raudive's original, are in reality just a form of simple radio receiver, not dissimilar to an old-fashioned crystal radio, and are therefore capable of picking up almost every nearby or sufficiently powerful radio transmission.

Some EVP experimenters place their recording devices inside an earthed (grounded) enclosure. This method is based upon the principle of the Faraday cage and is intended to shield the recorder from electromagnetic fields and radio signals. To be most effective, the enclosure should be made from metal or some other electrically conductive material and it must be properly connected to Earth (ground). Further precautions need to be taken to minimise the microphone cable from acting as a radio antenna by using a shielded type of microphone cable. These can often be identified by having three or more connecting pins.

A recent derivative of the radio method is known as the 'Estes method'; there are several variations of this method in use. Most use some form of radio EVP device but instead of the audio being sent to a loudspeaker for everyone to hear, the sound is listened to by a single person using headphones. The individual then says aloud what they believe it is that they are hearing. A significant drawback with this method is that it is subjective. It relies entirely upon an individual's interpretating what they hear and then deciding what to say. This method removes all of the objective value that may be gained by using equipment to record and evaluate any sounds which are received. Any results obtained using this method are untestable and unreliable; its use by investigators cannot be recommended.

13.3 *Devices intended to assist EVP experiments*

Recorder based EVP experiments remain popular with investigators of haunted locations, and the use of digital audio recorders has dramatically reduced the time previously needed to rewind and play back each EVP session in order for them to listen for a response. Some digital recorders have developed an extraordinary reputation for their ability to capture and record EVP. The mythology which has grown around some of these perfectly ordinary devices means that they have become highly sought after and can change hands for many hundreds of pounds on the secondary market.

Over recent years, a variety of digital recorders have appeared, with claims that they have been modified or adapted in order to make them more suitable or more sensitive for EVP experiments. Often, there is very little information indicating how they have been modified or what has been changed to make them better for recording EVP. An examination of several reveals them to be ordinary mass-produced, often inexpensive, devices with no obvious modifications made to either the components or to their mode of operation. Typically, the quality of the sound recordings these devices produce is far below what can be expected from better quality recorders designed and intended for use by podcasters, broadcasters and musicians.

Investigators who wish to carry out EVP experiments as a part of their overall investigation strategy are strongly advised to avoid buying any recorder which is promoted as being designed or modified especially for EVP. Instead, they should consider acquiring a good quality digital recorder from one of the reputable manufacturers. These often cost much less than their 'made for ghost hunting' counterparts and will almost always produce better quality recordings. They also have the additional benefit of being capable of making ordinary location sound recordings.

13.4 *EVP 'boxes' and Apps*

There have been a number of attempts to develop EVP equipment which allows the investigator to communicate in real-time, without the tedium of waiting to listening to a recording. The desire for an instantaneous response has led to a steady stream of devices being offered to investigators. Each new iteration of EVP technology comes accompanied by claims of extraordinary efficacy and many also come with a hefty price tag. The majority of these devices are supplied with very little information regarding their specifications or the components that are used. Many are home-made, supplied with vague operating instructions or perhaps only a link to a video showing the device being used by an investigator, who is successfully conversing with an apparent ghost or spirit.

The basic method for using these devices remains much as before; the investigator asks a series of questions and listens for a response to come from a loudspeaker. All of the current devices use some type of radio receiver as their primary means of allowing the voices to communicate. The audio from the radio receiver is then fed through a number of additional components which are used to process the sound in some way before it is sent to the loudspeaker. In a number of EVP devices, the sound processing is done using one or more guitar effect pedals. The rationale for using these items is never adequately explained; when explanations are provided, they are often contradictory.

The vague specifications and overall lack of information makes it impossible for the investigator to demonstrate that their recordings are the result of anything other than ordinary radio signals or electrical interference. Rather than any of these EVP devices providing the investigator with data that can be viewed dispassionately and objectively, the investigator is left with only a recording containing an assortment of sounds and noises. Therefore, it is impossible to recommend any of these EVP devices or suggest that they be used during an investigation.

There are also a number of EVP software Apps that are popular with owners of smartphones and tablet computers; some of these Apps emulate the operation or the appearance of physical devices. Whilst there are undoubted benefits from using a smartphone or tablet as an audio recorder, there is no indication that any of these dedicated EVP Apps offer any advantage for the investigator and their use cannot be condoned.

13.5 *Additional notes for EVP experiments*

Regardless of the method used to obtain the voices, it is likely that the investigator will rely upon an audio recording as evidence of their experiments. Making a recording for the purpose of conducting an EVP experiment is no different to making any other type of sound recording. The investigator's aim should always be to obtain the best possible recording with the lowest levels of unwanted noise and interference.

Setting up of the recorder and the microphone should be done in the same manner to that which is used for location sound recording. Automatic level and gain controls (ALC and AGC) should be turned off or set to their minimum level, as should any noise reduction or audio enhancement controls. Recording levels should be set to prevent distortion and causes of extraneous sounds e.g., excessive handling, should be reduced to a minimum.

The investigator is advised to always conduct a series of test recordings beforehand. This should be done at the place where the EVP session is to be conducted in order to determine the best position for the microphone in order that it can pick up both the person asking the questions and the source of any response, e.g., a loudspeaker. When using a radio receiver, there will often be a significant difference in the volume of AM and FM broadcasts. If it is planned to change between AM and FM stations during the same EVP session, carrying out test recordings at each of the wavebands and receiving modes that will be used is recommended.

During an EVP session, it is common for several of the participants to speak and ask questions at the same time; they may also say aloud what they believe they are hearing. This undesirable situation not only undermines the value of the experiment due to the likelihood of suggestibility affecting the participants, but it also creates practical difficulties for the investigator when they are listening back to the recording; making it much more difficult for them to discern who is saying what.

To avoid this and to assist the listener, only one person at a time should speak; the other participants or onlookers should be encouraged to remain silent until they are called upon to speak. Participants should also be discouraged from saying or discussing anything that they may hear or think that they are hearing and reminded that even whispering may be picked up by the recorder. It is often helpful for participants and onlookers to make a brief written note of anything which they believe they hear or which they consider to be relevant.

With any EVP experiment, especially those which use a radio, it is important that a proper record of the experiment is made. This should include the precise location of the experiment, details of the radio receiver and a comprehensive list of the frequencies or wavebands that were being used and the times that each was in use.

When evaluating the results of an EVP experiment the investigator should treat the recordings in the same way as any other recording made during the investigation. Section 14.5 of this guide specifically considers the evaluation of EVP recordings.

14 | Working with Sound Recordings

The first step after making a recording will invariably be for the investigator to listen to the recording that has been made. Except to occasionally check the proper operation of the recorder and microphone, the investigator should avoid listening to their recording during the investigation session. Doing so may cause the investigator, or others who are present, to make assumptions that could bias their opinion and change their subsequent actions throughout the remainder of the visit.

Recordings often contain something of interest; this may be an unexpected noise or a sound that the investigator is unable to identify. The recording may be noisy and indistinct but notwithstanding any technical problems, the recording is a strong indication that an acoustic event did take place and that it was recorded. Therefore, any sounds which cannot be immediately understood should be treated as being potentially significant.

14.1 *Always make a copy*

Prior to it being listened to, every recording (analogue and digital) should be copied and the unaltered original recording placed to one side. In most instances, analogue recordings will need to be transferred to a digital format at this stage to more easily allow examination of the recording to be made using a computer. If an analogue to digital copy is required, then the computer software should be set to record an uncompressed audio file with a sample rate of 44.1kHz or 48kHz at a bit depth of 16- or 24-bit. Digital recordings should always be transferred using the same sample rate and bit depth as the original recording device. The investigator should not be tempted to try and upscale the recording by using a higher sample rate or bit depth as it is impossible to add extra sound data after it has been recorded.

Once a digital copy has been made it should be always given a meaningful file name. This should contain a reference to the location and the date / time it was recorded. The investigator should now <u>only</u> use the copy for all subsequent actions. The original recording should be carefully retained until the investigator is either satisfied that the recording contains nothing of further interest or is able to safely archive it. If the original recording is on a removable media such as a memory card, this can simply be removed and stored.

With original recordings that were made using a device which has a non-removable memory, the investigator should make a copy using the same sample rate, bit-rate and file format as the original. This copy should be treated in the same manner as if it were the original recording. Wherever possible, the original recording should also be retained on the recording device's internal memory until the investigator has completed their consideration of the recording.

Following the creation of the working copy, the original recording should be listened to one final time, in its entirety, using the original recording device. They should then listen to the copy, on the computer or device which will be used for the examining the recording. This will highlight any problems which may have occurred during the copying process. These are more likely to happen with analogue recordings, but problems can sometimes occur with digital recordings.

It is recommended that the original recording, or those copies which are being considered in the same way as original audio recordings, should be retained and archived. The archived recordings can be used to provide a useful reference source and library of sounds which may be used when considering other recordings, either made at the same or another location.

The following guidance for reviewing and examining a recording should be only carried out using a <u>copy</u> of the original recording.

14.2 *Listening tests*

When the investigator is satisfied that the copy is an accurate representation of the original then it is suggested that it next be played to a number of people. Listeners should be provided with no information about the contents of the recording or what they should be listening for. Take care to avoid leading statements and questions such as "listen to this voice" or "can you hear footsteps in this recording?"

Whenever possible, listening tests should be carried out individually. Group listening tests carry a greater risk of someone inadvertently saying their thoughts out aloud and potentially changing or biasing the opinions of the other listeners.

At the commencement of the listening test, it is helpful to play a short (30 second) clip of sound which the investigator has determined contains nothing of interest. This allows the listener to attune their ear to the recordings they will be listening to. If it is not possible to edit a short clip from the actual recording, white noise played at a similar volume will often suffice.

To avoid the listener becoming bored or fatigued, keep listening sessions as short as possible. With longer recordings, this may require the recording to be edited, to remove any parts of the recording which contain nothing of interest. If recordings are edited, it is advisable to always leave a minimum lead-in of between five and ten seconds for each part of the recording that the listener has been asked to review and a similar amount of run-out time afterwards.

Immediately after each recording or part has been listened to, ask the listener to write down their comments and thoughts. This should be done straight away; the human memory for sound is short and unreliable. Listeners should not be allowed to subsequently change or edit their notes. Repeat this step for each section of the recording that is of interest.

When reviewing the comments of those participating in the listening tests, the investigator should consider all comments and should not disregard any comments which they themselves may disagree with or which are not supportive of either their own opinion or that of other listeners.

14.3 *Analysing the recordings*

Many investigators will wish to use a computer and sound editing software to listen to and adjust the recording in order to help them try to discern what it may contain. Often, they might set about changing the volume, playback speed and adjusting other parameters of the recording in order to do this, but this method should be avoided.

Forensic audio analysis is a highly specialist skill that requires extensive training and practise; expert analysts also have access to specially developed software to assist them. Ordinary sound editing software is unsuitable for conducting a forensic level of acoustic analysis, but with care it can be used to assist the investigator. For example, a recording which is noisy or difficult to understand can sometimes be improved sufficiently enough to allow the investigator to discern what the recording contains.

Every change that is undertaken using a computer will result in a permanent alteration of the initial recording. Therefore, whenever the investigator wishes to carry out any examination or alteration of the recording it is always advisable that they make and use an additional copy of the recording. Derived from the methods used by forensic audio analysts, the following method is recommended. The method will inevitably produce a number of files and folders and is sometimes a time-consuming process. Nevertheless, it allows every change which has been made to the recording to be followed and if necessary, replicated by anyone wishing to review the analysis or its conclusions and can also be used to support a conclusion when the results of the investigation are presented.

- Create a computer folder with a meaningful title that indicates the location and the date / time that the recording took place. Place a first-generation, unaltered copy of the recording into this folder; this will be your reference recording.

- Only ever change one variable or parameter of the sound at a time and save each change into the computer folder as a new audio file, giving each a meaningful filename or numbering sequence, e.g., *Soundvolume1.wav, Soundvolume2.wav* etc.

- It is important that every change that is made is documented. This can easily be done by creating a text file indicating the name and build number of the software that was used and listing every change made to the recording using their filenames, e.g., *Soundvolume1 – volume increased by 5%, Soundvolume2 – volume increased by a further 5%* etc. Save this text file in the folder created for the recording.

Occasionally, it may be helpful to apply more radical alterations to the recorded audio. These may include increasing or decreasing the playback speed or the selective use of frequency filtering. The use of any editing tools, the amount they have been applied and the order in which they were used should always be carefully documented by the investigator.

Software can only ever assist the investigator; it is incapable of determining what the sound recording is of, or represents. In every case, the final decision regarding a recording will be a subjective interpretation by the investigator. Their decision should draw together all of the available information relating to the recording. This includes the testimony of witnesses, the investigator's knowledge and experience of the location, the prevailing circumstances when the recording was made, and the results from the listening tests. The investigator should also consider the recording apparatus, its placement at the location and how it was operated, together with the manner in which the recording was subsequently handled and examined.

Following analysis or examination, the folder containing the copies and the notes should be retained and archived. This is particularly important with cases that are to be presented for review.

14.4 *The value of recording sound*

The investigator should remember that any recorded sound is just that; a recording of an acoustic event which actually took place. The recording on its own will rarely ever conclusively demonstrate the cause or the source of the sound. The value of stand-alone sound recording as part of the process for investigating a haunting or related phenomenon is therefore limited. Sometimes, a sound recording will be supported by additional information, including video footage, data from other measuring equipment and personal observations. In these instances, the recording will have a greater value; it may confirm, or contradict, a reported experience or some other event that occurred at the location.

14.5 *Evaluating EVP recordings*

Recordings which are made for the purpose of studying EVP should be treated in the same manner as ordinary sound recordings.

Investigators who carry out EVP experiments often concentrate their efforts towards trying to understand the words that they hear and record. Trying to discern and discover what has actually been heard and recorded during an EVP session is undoubtedly the most important part of the experiment. Whenever voices or other sounds are heard, the investigator must not overlook the importance of trying to ascertain their source and should always avoid an immediate assumption that the sounds are anomalous or that they cannot be ordinarily explained.

The notes made during the experiment relating to the frequencies and times they were being listened to, may provide valuable information. Radio broadcasts are normally scheduled and their frequencies and broadcast times are generally fixed and known. Speech and music on the recording can also be a helpful indicator, suggesting likely radio stations which may have been picked up. It is not unknown for unfamiliar foreign radio stations to be received many hundreds of miles and more from their source. This is most likely to occur at night, especially around dusk and dawn or throughout periods of settled fine weather. Therefore, the investigator may also find it helpful to consider the weather conditions that prevailed at the time of the EVP experiment.

Listening tests may be particularly helpful when trying to determine words or phrases. With EVP listening tests, it is important that each participant listens to the recordings separately and that they do not discuss them with any other participant until after all of the listening tests have been completed and the written notes have been collected.

The investigator should note occasions where the participants of the listening tests are in agreement regarding any words or phrases that they hear, but must also take equal note of those which do not agree or which appear to differ, even from the majority opinion.

In situations where there is widespread agreement that a voice can be heard and words or phrases can be identified, the investigator should not presume that this demonstrates any proof that the recording is of an anomalous event or that it has an anomalous cause. As with recordings of ordinary sounds the investigator must consider the evidence in its entirety.

14.6 *Submitted sound recordings*

It is not uncommon for an individual to submit a sound recording or EVP recording for the investigator to consider. This may be done to assist the investigator, but sometimes the sender is simply seeking validation for their recording; occasionally, they may use the investigator's comments in order to further their own claims about a location, their experiences or occasionally to promote their special abilities.

It is common for a person to send only one or two audio clips or examples, adding that they have many hours of similar material. It is unreasonable to expect the investigator to go through a large number of recordings, possibly comprising many hours of listening. However, it is often helpful to ask the sender to forward the entire sound recording that contains the clips they have selected. This will allow the investigator to listen to other portions of the recording which may provide a greater insight into the circumstances that prevailed at the time the recordings were made.

Oftentimes, the sound file will be sent using email or one of the social media messaging applications. These services normally apply data compression in order to make the file size smaller and also alter the recording; data compression will usually be applied without the sender and sometimes the investigator being aware that this has been used. The investigator should request a direct copy of the original file. This may necessitate the sender using a different file transfer method and selecting options to ensure the file is not compressed during the transfer. The investigator may need to advise the sender on how this ought to be done; senders may not be familiar with the steps that are required and these will vary depending on the file transfer service that is used.

Much of the examination procedure will be the same as that which the investigator uses to examine their own recordings. The same process of working with copies and documenting every step should be used. However, a submitted sound recording should always be given some additional scrutiny and subjected to some additional checks.

Submitted EVP recordings often include a transcript or some indication of what the sender thinks or believes is being said. This makes it much more difficult for the investigator to carry out an objective consideration of the recording. In these situations, the investigator is advised to ask another person, someone who is unaware of the transcript or comments, to carry out the examination of the recording. If there is no one who can do this, then it is often better for the investigator to decline the analysis or request additional material and emphasise that it should be sent without any comment or transcript.

14.6.1 *Look at the filename*

After a recording has been received, the first thing the investigator should look at is the file name. Some manufacturers use a sequential alphanumeric file numbering system; this sometimes indicates the manufacturer. If the recording does not conform to this system, for example it is called 'footsteps1.mp3', then this is a clear indication that the recording has been altered prior to being sent.

14.6.2 *Check the metadata*

Digital sound recordings normally contain an embedded metadata file. This holds information about when the original recording was made and the audio settings that were used. This should be checked and compared with the sender's description of the experience or the events. It is important to remember that not everyone will assiduously set the date and time on their recorder but the metadata can provide a lot of helpful additional information. Nevertheless, any inconsistency in the metadata may be an indication that the recording has been through one or more processes after it was made.

The investigator should be aware that audio metadata can be altered and added to, after the recording was made. This is to allow further information to be included, e.g., the title of the recording, the name of the composer or artist and additional copyright information. The metadata can also be used by playback software to present the listener with additional information about the recording.

If the recording has been edited or cut from a longer recording, the metadata will normally indicate an editing step has been applied. However, some audio editing software allows changes to be made to the date or time information, making it possible to hide any later editing or processing that may have taken place. Some of these alterations and changes to audio metadata may be difficult to detect without using sophisticated forensic software.

If the investigator suspects that the metadata contains any inconsistencies or alterations, they should compare this with the metadata of the full-length recording, if this is already been requested. If this is not available or the person claims that the recording they have supplied has not been changed or edited, the investigator should be cautious about proceeding with the examination. If the investigator decides to continue; they should note in their comments or report that the metadata was either absent or it contained inconsistencies.

15 | Photography

A camera is now considered to be an essential item of equipment in every investigation kit. Almost without exception, cameras now use a digital image sensor in place of the film and a computer instead of the darkroom and chemical developing processes. With the proliferation of camera-phones there are few investigators who do not have immediate access to a camera whenever they visit a location. For the majority of photographic situations, pictures taken using a camera-phone or a compact camera will usually be perfectly suitable and it is always better to have some type of camera available, than to have none at all.

In recent years still photography has given way to video as the preferred means of capturing visual evidence during an investigation, but photography remains popular and photographs which purport to show evidence of ghostly or paranormal phenomena are highly prized by investigators. Historically, photography has provided some of the most contentious and challenging evidence offered by investigators and has created much debate between those with opposing points of view. Digital photography has significantly worsened this situation; the ease with which a digital image can be edited or manipulated means that its value as evidence has become considerably less. Despite these problems, the camera remains one of the most useful pieces of equipment that the investigator can use, but greater care than ever must now be employed by investigators to ensure that their pictures help, rather than hinder, the investigation process.

Investigators are more likely to use a camera to take pictures at a time when they believe an anomaly may exist, for example, when someone reports seeing or experiencing something unusual. Undoubtedly, taking pictures at the time someone reports seeing an apparition or some other visual phenomenon is important and the resulting photograph may reveal something helpful. However, the real value of a camera is its ability to document and record the location in its normal state. Photographs are a useful memory aid, and allows the investigator to establish a baseline, fixing the position of objects and individuals in time and in-situ. For example, there may be instances when a person claims that an object has been moved, where an examination of earlier photographs can be used to confirm or refute this claim. Photography also lets the investigator test the sightlines of reported experiences; could the person have actually seen what they claim to have observed from their position?

Important Note: Many camera-phones and some cameras are able to automatically add a geo-tag to every picture which they take. This indicates the precise location where the picture was taken, often to within a few feet. Geo-tagging can sometimes be helpful, but its use by investigators should always be carefully considered. In some situations, it may compromise the confidentiality of the investigation or of a witness, especially if the images are subsequently presented in a public forum. The geo-tagging option can normally be turned off, but some devices may switch it back on when they themselves are turned on. Investigators should also ensure that each member of their team takes care to set the geo-tagging option correctly.

15.1 *Choosing a camera*

The majority of investigators will already have a camera built-in to their mobile phone; nevertheless, many prefer to use a separate camera. This will often be a compact digital camera, or sometimes a more advanced model such as a digital single lens reflex (DSLR). When selecting a camera, the investigator should always consider their own particular requirements and compare these to the various camera options that are available. The value of having a camera-phone readily to hand must also be balanced against the improved picture quality which can be achieved from a more dedicated device.

Prior to using any camera for the purposes of an investigation, the user should fully acquaint themselves with the operation of camera, paying particular attention to the modes and functions that they are most likely to use. With some camera-phones, further options and greater control of the camera's functions can often be obtained by using a separate photo App rather than the camera software provided by the camera-phone maker.

It is recommended that investigators take a series of practise pictures under conditions which are similar to those which they commonly find at investigation sites in order to fully familiarise themselves with the operation of the camera and the appearance of the resulting photographs.

15.2 *Automatic and user-controlled functions*

Fully automated picture taking is the default option for some cameras. This mode is designed to allow a picture of reasonable quality to be taken under the majority of circumstances. Software is used to control the focus, the exposure and all of the other settings; the user only needs to frame the picture and press the shutter.

Investigators often need to take photographs in situations when optimal photographic conditions don't exist. Under these conditions, the camera's automation can sometimes struggle and pictures will often be unsatisfactory. For instance, in low light, the camera may use a slow shutter speed, which frequently causes blurring, due to either the camera or the subject moving during the exposure. Alternatively, some cameras take a series of pictures, which are combined by the camera's software to produce the final image. This can also result in a number of unusual effects appearing in the final picture, particularly when there was any movement, either by the camera or within the scene, when the sequence of pictures was taken.

Even when the location is brightly lit, the automation may struggle to produce a properly exposed picture. There may be regions of deep shadow or a picture may be taken towards a bright light source. In these situations, some cameras will automatically take a series of pictures, each at a slightly different exposure setting, combining them to make the final image. The software is attempting to balance the dynamic range of the lighting conditions, but taking multiple shots can result in some unusual effects appearing in the final image.

Users should always consult their instruction manual and undertake a series of tests in order to familiarise themselves with the way that the automatic shooting modes operate. If options to take manual control of the camera are provided, these should also be tested and their use considered.

Almost every camera has a built-in clock and before every investigation, the correct setting of date and time should be checked and if necessary adjusted. It is easy to overlook this step, especially following a seasonal time change. This may not seem as important when using a camera-phone, which automatically updates its internal clock. Nevertheless, it should still be checked as occasional software and system errors can occur, resulting in the date and time being incorrectly recorded.

15.2.1 Controlling the exposure

Despite all of the automation, the basic process of photography remains unchanged since its invention. Light from the scene is focussed by a lens onto a sensitive strip of film or a digital sensor. The amount of light that is required to make a good exposure is dictated by the sensitivity of the film or sensor, and is regulated using a combination of two controls, the shutter and the aperture.

15.2.2 Film and sensor sensitivity

The sensitivity of film is fixed at manufacture, and is a function of the size and the density of light sensitive silver-halide crystals across the surface of the film. The sensitivity is referred to by an ISO (International Standards Organisation) number; the higher the number the more sensitive the film is to light.

The optimal sensitivity of a digital sensor is also fixed at manufacture. Digital sensors use the same ISO numbering system to represent their light sensitivity. Unlike film, digital sensors can be made to operate over a range of sensitivities by altering the amount of amplification that is applied to the sensor's output signal; the optimal sensitivity of a sensor is normally indicated by the lowest ISO value that is available. In low light, increased levels of amplification can cause unwanted artefacts and image noise to appear in the final picture.

15.2.3 Shutter speed and aperture

The amount of light that is needed to produce a properly exposed photograph is determined by the sensitivity of the sensor (or film). To control the amount of light reaching the sensor, the camera uses a combination of the shutter speed and aperture size. The shutter is a mechanism which allows light to reach the sensor for a controlled period of time. The shutter may be either a mechanical device which can be quickly opened and closed, or an electronic switch that turns the sensor's output on and off. The aperture is an opening, through which the light passes before reaching the sensor. The size of the aperture may be varied in order to control the amount of light reaching the sensor or to adjust the depth of focus. In some basic cameras, the aperture is fixed and cannot be changed. In these circumstances, a combination of the shutter speed and altering the sensitivity of the sensor are used to control the exposure.

Even with the steadiest of hands, it is difficult to take a picture without motion blur at shutter speeds slower than about 1/30th of a second. Cameras which are fully automated may select a very slow shutter speed; for example, slower than 1/15th of a second, often without the user's knowledge. Using a tripod or some other supporting surface will significantly reduce the likelihood of camera motion blur occurring. If there are no options to use a tripod or other support, then a usable picture may be obtained by increasing the ISO of the sensor until a faster shutter speed is available; it is always easier to discern detail in a noisy image than in an image that has motion blurring.

15.3 *The sensor*

There are several factors relating to the sensor that investigators may wish to consider. Specifically, these are the size of the individual pixels, the number of pixels and the overall size of the sensor. The size of the individual pixels is the most important; larger pixels have a greater light gathering ability and consequently the sensor's output requires less amplification and produces fewer image artefacts. The total number of pixels is less important; more pixels can allow finer detail to be recorded by the sensor but can introduce image noise which may obscure the additional detail. For any given number of pixels, sensors that are physically larger will always have bigger pixels and will always produce better quality pictures, especially in poorer lighting conditions. Camera-phones and many compact cameras typically use a small sensor, although an increasing number of compact cameras and all DSLR's use sensors that are physically larger with correspondingly bigger pixels.

15.4 *The Lens*

The importance of the lens should not be overlooked. The purpose of the lens is to bring all of the available light into focus on the sensor in order to produce sharp images which reveal the greatest amount of detail. Objects which are not in focus may appear to be indistinct and are sometimes the cause of reported paranormal anomalies in pictures. A typical lens is constructed using a number of individual lens elements made from optical plastic or glass. Some, or all of the lens elements will be chemically coated to reduce reflections and refractions within the lens or to assist the passage of certain wavelengths of light (colours). Lenses are normally described by reference to their focal length or to their field of view, e.g., wide-angle, telephoto or zoom.

15.4.1 *Focal length and field of view*

The field of view is determined by the physical size of the sensor and the focal length of the lens (expressed in millimetres). The lower the focal length value, the wider will be the field of view; conversely, the higher the focal length, the narrower will be the field of view. The field of view of a lens may be fixed or variable. The field of view is expressed using degrees of arc of a circle. Some manufacturers state this as a diagonal (corner to corner) measurement, whilst others prefer to use a horizontal value.

Wide angle lenses have a field of view that typically exceeds 40°. At very wide angles, the lens has to increasingly bend the peripheral light inwards towards the sensor which can cause the edges of the picture to become distorted. This is especially noticeable with straight lines, which become increasingly curved the further from the centre of the image they lie. Telephoto lenses have a narrower field of view, ordinarily less than 30°, this has the effect of magnifying the scene, thereby allowing more distant objects to be photographed. The narrow field of view can be useful for isolating parts of a scene, but most investigators will often find a wide-angle lens is preferable to a telephoto lens.

Zoom lenses which have a moderate optical zoom range of 2x or 3x may be the most helpful, allowing the investigator to photograph either a wider viewpoint or concentrate upon objects of interest without having to change either the lens or their position. Zoom lenses also suffer from image distortion. This becomes particularly pronounced at the edges and corners of the picture and increases as the field of view widens. In addition to the optical zoom, a number of cameras also provide a digital zoom. This electronically enlarges the image, but using the digital zoom will always cause a reduction in the image quality. If the investigator needs to enlarge any part of an image, better results will often be obtained afterwards using a computer and photo editing software.

15.4.2 *Focus and depth of field*

The region of the image which is in focus is called the depth of field. It is variable depending upon the size of the aperture and the focal length of the lens.

Focussing is often automated; the camera uses software algorithms to focus upon what it determines is the most important item in the scene, and investigators may sometimes find that the camera continually tries to focus on unwanted parts of the scene. Cameras are designed for a consumer market and the software prioritises certain elements e.g., people and faces, when choosing a point of focus. Auto-focus is generally reliable but it can struggle to operate in low light or in situations where there are poor levels of contrast between different objects. In these situations, the option to focus manually is an advantage, but one that is frequently overlooked by investigators. Focussing is normally done by moving some of the elements inside the lens back and forth.

Some basic cameras do not need to focus; these are referred to as fixed focus or focus-free. Fixed focus cameras combine a wide-angle lens with a small fixed aperture, in order to give an extended depth of field. Generally, everything from one or two feet in front of the camera will appear to be in focus; objects closer than this will increasingly appear out of focus. The loss of focus becomes more pronounced the nearer to the camera the object is; distant objects will always remain in focus. Because of the fixed aperture, the exposure can only be controlled by altering the shutter speed or changing the sensitivity of the sensor. Focus-free cameras often perform badly in low light, and are more likely to require the use of additional light, normally using the camera's flash.

15.5 *Image Compression and file formats*

Almost every camera offers a range of options for setting the picture quality and the amount of digital compression that is applied. These options are only provided in order to reduce the file size and increase the number of pictures that can be stored in the camera's memory. Any reduction in quality or the use of increased compression will always result in a loss of picture detail which can never be restored.

In most cameras the default file format is the 'jpeg' (.jpg) which is a compressed format. Normally several levels of compression can be selected; these are often referred to as the image quality settings. Selecting the lowest amount of compression, i.e., the highest quality, will produce larger file sizes but more of the image data will be retained. Some cameras allow the user to shoot using a RAW file format. This format is essentially the unprocessed data from the sensor. Images shot using this format require additional processing to be carried out; this is normally done afterwards using a computer. Using the RAW format may offer several significant advantages for the investigator. None of the original image data is lost, and the detail in regions of the picture that are overly dark can be recovered. In low light, using the RAW format will often result in a sharper, clearer image but the RAW format will not correct for any motion blur. RAW file sizes are considerably larger than those which use a compressed format and the processing that is required afterwards can be time consuming.

Investigators are advised to select either a non-compressed file format or choose the lowest amount of compression and the highest picture quality that is available. If they find that the camera's memory is becoming full, they may either swap to a fresh memory card or download the pictures in order to free up space for further pictures to be taken.

Wherever possible the picture storage media should be re-formatted before every investigation visit in order to completely remove previous images. For camera-phones which store their pictures onto the device's internal memory, re-formatting may not be possible but the investigator should be aware that simply deleting and erasing a picture may not always completely remove the image information and it is not unknown for a previously taken and erased picture to partially reappear in pictures taken sometime later.

15.6 *Flash and additional lighting*

In situations where the lighting conditions are poor or difficult, it may be necessary to add extra light; often this is by means of a built-in flash or light emitting diode (LED). However, using this type of lighting can create problems for the investigator.

The built-in flash is often located close to the lens axis. The close proximity of the light source to the lens axis can result in some of the light being reflected back off nearby objects, such as airborne dust particles, insects and water droplets and causing bright spots to appear in the picture. These bright spots are commonly referred to as orbs by some investigators and there are many who contend that they represent some type of paranormal phenomenon. Orbs are more likely to occur when using a compact camera and several manufacturers now include information about this frequently observed phenomenon in their instruction manuals. Another commonly observed phenomenon which may be caused by the reflected light from the flash is the appearance of unusual streaks and patches of light in the picture. Due to the intensity of the light, reflections can sometimes even occur from surfaces or objects which may not normally be considered as being reflective. The intense light from the flash can also result in pictures which contain regions of dense shadow that has little or no detail. It is also not uncommon for fingers, camera straps or other items to partially obscure the flash and cause unexpected shadows to appear in the pictures.

In some designs, especially camera-phones, the flash is located adjacent to the lens which often protrudes slightly from the body of the device. This arrangement can sometimes result in unusual effects appearing in the picture. This is a particular problem if the lens is dirty or covered in finger prints or when the phone's protective case does not have sufficient space around the flash, allowing some of the light to be directed towards the lens.

In some modes, the camera may fire the flash, even when the ambient lighting seems sufficiently bright for non-flash photography. When the flash is used, the camera may also select a different shutter speed and aperture to that which the user is expecting. This can result in the photograph containing elements which appear unnatural.

In situations where additional light from the flash is not required, it is recommended that it is turned off. In some cameras, the use of the flash is determined entirely by the software with no option to turn it off. Selecting a higher ISO setting for the sensor can sometimes allow pictures to be taken without the camera resorting to using the flash.

Using a light that is mounted further from the lens can reduce many of these problems and is often a more controllable way to illuminate a scene. The light can be mounted to the camera using an accessory mount or it can be moved off the camera entirely onto a separate support. Some types of accessory lighting allow the user to aim the lighting upwards or to the side which reduces the amount of direct frontal lighting. This reduces the harshness of the illumination and may also improve the definition of objects within the scene. However, it can produce shadows beneath or to the side of objects, which in some instances can appear to be unusual.

15.7 *Modified cameras*

In recent years, investigators have increasingly begun to use cameras which claim to provide additional capabilities that some may consider to be desirable, and there are a number of adaptions and modifications which are promoted as being specifically for paranormal investigation use. The majority of these modifications alter the sensor's sensitivity to either infra-red or ultraviolet light. This modification is supported by a widespread belief that extending the range of the sensor makes it possible to capture evidence of paranormal phenomena that cannot ordinarily be photographed.

By design, digital sensors are inherently more sensitive than the human eye to infra-red (IR) light; they are also slightly more sensitive to ultraviolet (UV) light. For normal picture taking, both of these non-visible frequencies of light need to be properly controlled in order to produce satisfactory pictures without unusual colour casts and other anomalies appearing in the picture. The unwanted IR light is normally blocked by using a filter placed immediately in front of the sensor. The most common ghost hunting modification simply involves removing this filter, thereby increasing the amount of infra-red light reaching the sensor.

Unwanted UV light is controlled by chemical coatings applied to the lens surface and by the inherent UV light absorbing properties of the material used to make the lens elements. Sensitivity to UV light cannot be altered, except by removing the lens coating, which is a difficult process and any gains from doing so are likely to be insignificant, as the individual lens elements are often entirely made from ultraviolet absorbing materials.

Photographs taken with modified cameras may often lack fine detail and appear less distinct overall, as the lens is unable to bring all of the light frequencies into correct focus on the sensor. Additionally, the camera's software is designed to produce pictures from an unmodified sensor and any modifications are more likely to result in image anomalies being produced by the software. So far, none of these ghost hunting modifications have been shown to provide any significant advantages to the investigator. Nevertheless, these cameras remain a popular choice with investigators.

It is also possible to take still photographs with some of the video cameras which have an IR (night) shooting mode. There are also a number of specialist modifiers who are able to convert an ordinary digital camera for those who wish to take IR photographs for a variety of non-paranormal reasons. Either of these options can provide the investigator with an ability to take pictures under conditions of apparent visual darkness. However, image anomalies may still be present; these are especially likely in situations when the location is lit by a mix of visible and IR lighting. The mixed lighting exacerbates the problem of bringing the full range of light frequencies to a common point of focus at the sensor. This situation can often be easily resolved by the fitting of an IR pass filter. This is fitted in front of the lens, blocking the unwanted visible light and only allowing IR light to reach the sensor. Filters are available in various strengths in order to selectively block unwanted parts of the visible light spectra, labelled according to the frequency above which they allow light to pass. For example, an IR75 allows only IR light above 750 nanometres to pass unhindered and an IR90 passes all IR light above 900 nanometres. These filters are inexpensive and often available in a range of values allowing the investigator to select the most appropriate for the prevailing conditions and the type of IR lighting they may be using. The filters themselves, depending upon the quality of the material and the manufacturer, may introduce small amounts of degradation or distortions into the picture.

Consumer night-shot video cameras are designed to only have a very restricted range of shutter speeds and apertures available when operating in their IR picture and video operating modes. Picture taking can be improved by the use of an IR pass filter but the slow shutter speeds and wide apertures which must be used, makes them unsuitable for capturing movement without significant motion blur and may restrict the depth of focus.

16 | Video Photography – Videography

The use of video has only been commonplace in investigations since the late 1990's, but in recent years it has become the predominant means for obtaining and presenting evidence of apparently paranormal phenomena. In many circumstances, videography can be advantageous; for instance, it allows the investigator to record moving images and sound simultaneously which may provide them with important additional information and context that is not possible with photography or sound recording alone.

Videography shares many similarities and operating characteristics with still photography; both types of camera use the same type of image sensor and have similar methods for controlling the focus and the exposure. Users of video cameras are therefore advised to also read Section 15 of these notes.

The image resolution of video images is significantly lower than with still photographs. The most common video resolution in use, 1080 high definition (HD) video, has a resolution of 1,920 x 1,080 pixels, which is 2.1 million pixels (2.1 Megapixels). This is far below the resolution of even moderate consumer cameras and camera-phones which can easily manage a resolution of 3,872 x 2,592 pixels (10 Megapixels) or greater.

Nowadays, almost every consumer camera and camera-phone is capable of taking good quality video footage and there are numerous other video camera options including multi-camera CCTV systems and body-worn action cameras.

As with every item of equipment, the decision to use video as part of the investigation process should always be governed by the nature of the reported phenomena and the circumstances under which they occur. There may be instances where there is no requirement to use videography or when its use would serve little useful purpose. Sometimes, videography can become detrimental to the investigation process; it is not unusual to see investigators staring intently at a camera screen or CCTV monitor, barely ever looking up at their surroundings. In the presence of a video camera some participants including witnesses and investigators can become overly self-aware and alter their usual actions or behaviour.

Important Note: Many camera-phones and some video cameras are able to automatically add a geo-tag to every video which they take. This indicates the precise location where the video was taken, often to within a few feet. Geo-tagging can sometimes be helpful, but its use by investigators should always be carefully considered. In some situations, it may compromise the confidentiality of the investigation or of a witness, especially if the images are subsequently presented in a public forum. The geo-tagging option can normally be turned off, but some devices will switch it back on when they themselves are turned on. Investigators should also ensure that each member of their team takes care to set the geo-tagging option correctly.

16.1 *Choosing a video camera*

Investigators have a wide range of video cameras and systems to choose from and the decision regarding which to choose and to use is not always straightforward. Different locations and changing situations may require the use of different types of video camera in order to obtain the best quality footage. A camera-phone is often the most readily to hand, providing almost instantaneous availability and reasonable performance. Consumer level camcorders are a popular choice, with models that range from fully automated entry level devices to semi-professional cameras with enhanced features, and options for obtaining high quality footage in almost every type of situation. Security camera systems and action cameras are also popular, allowing the investigator to set-up multiple camera views or to wear body-mounted, for first person, point-of-view (POV) footage. In recent years, investigators have also started to use video cameras that have various modifications and adaptions which claim to enhance the camera's ability to visualise paranormal phenomena.

16.2 *User operated controls*

The degree of user control varies greatly depending upon the video camera model.

Security cameras often only have a small amount of manual control; for instance, the user may only be able to change the overall exposure / brightness. Camera-phones allow a greater degree of control over the resolution, exposure and focus, but accessing the various settings may not be straightforward and in some models these options may only be accessible by using additional Apps. This may prove to be time consuming and many simply leave the camera on the fully automated settings, which seldom provide the best possible video footage, especially under difficult lighting conditions. Body worn action cameras also offer a range of options but these are often aimed towards their primary purpose of recording first person and POV video with restricted options for controlling the exposure or the focus.

Many of the operating controls of a video camera are similar to those of a still camera, although they are sometimes labelled in different ways by different manufacturers. Before any investigation use, the user should fully acquaint themselves with all of the controls and the modes which they are likely to require.

For the majority of the time, the video camera's default settings will provide acceptable video quality under moderate lighting conditions, indoors or outside.

16.2.1 *Lens and focusing*

In most regards, the lens of a video camera is identical to that which is fitted to any other type of camera. With the exception of expensive broadcast cameras, video camera lenses usually provide only limited options to directly control the lens aperture or depth of field. A video camera lens will often have a large optical zoom range; often, 10x or more. This is a useful option for controlling the field of view or concentrating upon particular areas of interest within the location. Many video cameras also have a digital zoom option that may offer very large amounts of image magnification. Digital zooms always degrade the image quality and should not be used. Wherever possible, they should be turned off to prevent any inadvertent use.

Action cameras and models with a very wide field of view may use a fixed focus lens with no user control. Automatic focus is common on consumer video cameras, sometimes with only limited options for manual control. Video cameras which have automatic focussing may occasionally cause problems in some situations, especially under poor lighting conditions. Unlike a still camera which only needs to focus for a brief period of time whilst a photograph is taken, the auto-focussing system in a video camera is always on and constantly searching for the correct point of focus. This may result in the image periodically going in and out of focus, or suddenly changing the point of focus entirely onto something else within the scene. If this occurs, the user should switch to manual control of the focus. If this option is not provided then it may be necessary increase the levels of illumination within the scene to allow the focussing system to operate more effectively.

Many video cameras provide some form of image stabilisation; this may be electronic or optical. Image stabilisation can be very effective in some situations but camera manufacturers recommend that it should be turned off whenever the camera is being used on a tripod or other fixed mount. Leaving it on may cause the footage to appear to wobble or move as the system continually searches for an optimal position.

16.2.2 *Image definition*

The most common video resolution is currently 1080 High Definition (HD), whilst the highest consumer resolution is 4K Ultra-High Definition (UHD); this has a pixel resolution of 3,840 x 2,160 (about 8.2 megapixels). Ultra-high definition might be considered excessive in some investigation situations but it can be helpful in situations where the investigator needs to zoom into portions of the footage. Using 4K UHD, it is possible to enlarge any part of the scene up to a magnification of 4x with no significant loss of detail; the zoomed footage will have a resolution of 1080 HD. In many situations a resolution of 1080 HD will be perfectly adequate, allowing a good amount of detail to be retained even in slightly enlarged portions of the footage. Resolutions lower than 1080 HD are still common for security cameras and some basic camcorders. Typically, these may have a resolution of 1,280 x 720 pixels (720) or sometimes even lower. Confusingly, 720, is also referred to as high definition (HD) by some camera makers. Wherever possible, the investigator should avoid cameras with resolutions that are lower than 720 and carefully check the specifications of any camera marked only as being 'HD' quality, especially less expensive or older models.

16.2.3 *Video compression and compatibility*

Video produces a lot of data and almost every video system requires some form of data compression to optimise the video storage memory. Data compression is particularly necessary in the case of streamed video and cloud storage. A number of video file formats are used by camera makers and internet connected systems. Unfortunately, not all of the formats that are in use are compatible with one another and options to change the format may be limited. Many investigators will use the default options, but these may not always provide the best possible video footage. Wherever possible the investigator should try to ensure that their video footage is of the highest possible quality. They should consult the user manual or online instructions (in the case of video streaming cloud services) for options that are available.

16.2.4 *Frame rate*

In addition to the usual exposure controls, i.e., shutter speed and aperture, video cameras have two further ways in which the footage can be adjusted; these are the frame rate and method by which the image data is collected (scanned) from the sensor by the image processor.

Video footage is actually a series of still pictures, taken rapidly in a sequence. The number of individual pictures that are taken every second is the frame rate, expressed in frames per second (fps). Cinematic films use a frame rate of 24fps which approximates to the slowest speed at which the human eye sees the individual frames as continual motion. Video cameras and camera-phones normally use a default frame rate of 30fps but some allow the user to select a higher frame rate, which will be a multiple of the default frame rate, e.g., 60fps, 120fps and 240fps. The default 30fps frame rate provides better low-light performance but it can result in motion blurring which may be particularly noticeable if objects in the scene are moving quickly or if the camera is moved rapidly. Choosing a frame rate of 60fps is generally a good basis for most types of videography, particularly in brighter lighting conditions. Higher frame rates may be useful if the user wishes to freeze motion or to play back footage more smoothly in slow motion. The higher frame rates, e.g., 120fps and 240fps require brighter lighting conditions in order to produce properly exposed footage and so are not particularly useable in low-light situations.

A note regarding frame rate is necessary for investigators using night-vision video cameras and security CCTV cameras; these often have a default frame rate of 15fps or slower in order to extract the most from the low levels of lighting that are available. This can introduce serious motion blurring around any object which is moving and is the frequent cause of many claimed paranormal phenomena seen on videos.

A final consideration when using video is the method by which the raw information captured by the sensor is read by the image processor. This becomes more significant in situations when it is necessary to capture still images from the video footage. Two methods are available; progressive scan, indicated using a lower case 'p' after the resolution, e.g., 1080p, and interleaved scan, which uses a lower case 'i' after the resolution e.g., 1080i. Progressive scan is more memory and processor intensive but provides better quality still images and is becoming more common as image processors become more powerful. Screen captures or stills from interleaved video footage is normally composed of two interleaved frames taken fractions of a second apart which can cause softening and a loss of definition. Some cameras offer both options and investigators are advised to use progressive scanning whenever possible.

16.2.5 *Storage and memory*

The way in which the video camera records and stores the footage can also influence the investigator's options and decisions. Recordings may be stored on an internal memory which may be fixed or removeable; some cameras also allow the footage to be sent to an external hard drive, connected to the camera. The most recent innovations allow videos to be uploaded wirelessly either for storage or to be streamed live using one of a number of services including YouTube and Facebook. The investigator may wish to continuously record for many hours which is difficult to undertake with cameras that use an internal memory or memory card; in these circumstances external storage might be a better option. Some models with an internal memory have a provision for attaching an external memory storage device and security camera systems (CCTV) can provide very long recording times, some being able to record continuously for many days, weeks or even months.

Unless the investigator specifically needs to leave the camera recording for long periods then it is almost always better to periodically download the recordings and clear the memory. If the camera uses an internal memory, video files can be downloaded from the camera to free additional space. For cameras that have removeable memory cards, it is recommended to use cards with a lower capacity instead of a single card of greater capacity. For example, using several 32Gb cards rather than a single 128Gb card affords greater protection in the event of an individual memory card becoming damaged or ceasing to work correctly; only a proportion of the footage will be lost. With fixed memory cameras, regular downloading also protects the footage from any subsequent failure or loss.

To prevent older recordings from appearing through later recordings it is important to ensure that the memory is fully cleared by reformatting the memory media. For video cameras that use tape then it is recommended that each tape is fully erased by using a tape-eraser and that each tape is used no more than four or five times for the purposes of investigating. Tapes which have been used previously can still be used for recording interviews.

16.3 *Additional Lighting*

In some situations, it may be necessary to add extra illumination. Usually, the simplest way to do this is to turn on the lighting within the location. However, this is not always possible and an accessory video light may be needed. A small number of video cameras do have a built-in light but this is generally a weak affair, suitable only for illuminating the scene a few feet in front of the camera.

Video lights now predominantly use light emitting diode (LED) technology which can be powered either by the camera, an independent battery in the lamp or the electricity supply. Video lights are often extremely bright and create harsh shadows. They may be necessary in order to produce a good quality image but their intensity can significantly impair a person's ability to see in lower lighting conditions. It is often better to aim the light upwards or to the side, in order to bounce some of the light off a ceiling or wall. This will usually still provide a useable level of lighting for the video camera but is less dazzling to anyone who is in front of the camera.

16.3.1 *Difficult lighting conditions and infra-red videography*

Visual phenomena are often reported in difficult lighting situations, under which a video camera might struggle. Using a video camera which has specific low-light modes may sometimes be the only suitable means available for the investigator to capture video footage. Some video cameras provide extremely low-light capabilities or the ability to operate in conditions of near darkness. This is done using one of two methods: by amplifying the available light or by using infra-red (IR) illumination.

Light amplification cameras (image intensifiers) are an

expensive option and are rarely used by investigators, most preferring to use an IR sensitive camera that exploits the inherent sensitivity of the digital sensor to IR light. In the absence of visible light, these cameras use an IR illumination source. This can either be a built-in IR light emitting diode (LED) or some other external IR light source. The IR illumination is almost invisible to the naked eye but it can be used to produce footage of a reasonable quality in conditions that appear completely dark to the observer. In order for the IR mode to function properly, the camera must have the IR blocking filter removed. This is located immediately in front of the sensor and blocks IR light reaching the sensor and creating unnatural and unwanted colour casts in visible light footage; in some consumer cameras, this is a user selected option. When this mode is selected the camera will also automatically adjust the exposure and the framerate in order to ensure the best quality footage. Many security camera designs omit the IR filter entirely and make use of either monochrome or software corrected colour, depending upon the ambient lighting conditions, in order to avoid the problems created by the lack of an IR filter.

Infra-red videography has several drawbacks which the investigator needs to be aware of. The main problem which arises is caused by the wavelength of the IR light being different to the wavelengths of visible light. In mixed lighting conditions, the lens is unable to properly focus the available visible light and IR light resulting in the characteristically soft footage that is often seen from cameras when using this mode. In conditions where the IR mode is being used in mixed lighting, this focussing problem can often be improved by fitting an IR pass filter to the front of the camera lens. This blocks out the wavelengths of visible light, but IR light is able to pass unhindered, allowing the camera's focussing mechanism to bring the scene into sharper focus. This appears almost opaque to the naked eye, but IR light can pass unhindered. Ideally, a filter should be chosen that most closely matches the wavelength of the IR light that is being used. Most IR LED illumination has a wavelength of around 750nm – 850nm, therefore an IR75 (750nm) or IR85 (850nm) will provide the best results. If the wavelength of the IR light isn't known, a 700nm (IR70) filter will always work, removing almost all of the visible light. Note: The IR pass filter should always be removed when using the camera in visible lighting, otherwise footage will either be too dark or excessively noisy as the camera will be forced to use greatly increased levels of signal amplification in order to produce an image.

16.4 *Sound recording*

The importance of recording sound is often overlooked by video users. The addition of sound is one of the key advantages that video offers to the investigator. The incorporation of sound recording alongside the pictures provides a significant level of additional information and context which can provide a greater insight and understanding of the overall situation. The microphones that are built into camcorders are usually quite basic, with little user control, whilst security cameras may not have any form of sound recording or may sometimes have just a rudimentary microphone. Built-in microphones may suffice in some quiet indoor situations but a video camera that allows the user to connect a better-quality external microphone is a better choice. If options for altering the way in which sound is recorded are provided then the investigator should use these to select the highest quality and the lowest audio compression.

The section of these guidance notes relating to sound recording and microphones provides additional information about microphones and further guidance regarding audio quality and compression techniques which are also applicable to sound recording in videography (see **Secs. 11 and 12**).

16.5 *Batteries and power*

Another of the problems that investigators often encounter when using video cameras is the requirement to provide sufficient battery power. Camera makers rarely supply a battery that lasts much over thirty or forty minutes of recording time, often much less depending upon the environment and the camera options which are selected. The addition of microphones and lights which draw their power from the camera will also significantly reduce the recording time. Additional batteries can be purchased, but these can be an expensive option. Many cameras allow the use of some form of external power, either by means of the electricity supply or by means of connecting a large external battery pack. External power options may impair the mobility of the camera but whenever the camera is used in a fixed position, external power options should be considered and used wherever possible. Battery care should not be overlooked and is discussed in more detail in section 4.3 of this guide.

In order to provide a useful safety margin, it is recommended that both battery and memory capacity are sufficient to last at least double the planned investigation duration. In colder conditions, battery life may be considerably reduced. It is also worthwhile considering using a separate external power supply wherever possible.

16.6 *Video anomalies caused by the camera settings*

There are a number of common video anomalies which can be caused by a mismatch between the frame rate and the shutter speed and which have been presented as paranormal phenomena from time to time. Videographers describe these anomalies collectively as rolling shutter effects and give them various descriptive names such as wobble, skew, spatial aliasing and temporal aliasing. Straight objects can appear to bend or curve and in some extreme instances, objects may even seem to partially disappear and reappear in the footage.

These effects are most likely to be noticed when either the camera or objects within the scene are moving rapidly or when the lighting abruptly changes. Most video cameras are likely to suffer from these rolling shutter effects occasionally. Rolling shutter problems are notoriously difficult to correct and investigators should be aware of this issue whenever they are attempting to take video of rapidly moving objects or in situations where they are quickly moving the camera around such as in point of view handheld footage which is popular with many investigators. Flickering is also a common problem; this is caused by the frame rate of the camera being the same or faster than the frequency of the lighting. This is particularly observable with fluorescent tubes and some LED's. The strobing effect can result in footage becoming difficult to watch and for some individuals may cause them to feel unwell.

16.7 *Specialist use video cameras*

Several video camera models are available which are designed to be used particular situations or for specialist applications. These include action cameras and 360° view panoramic cameras.

Action cameras are small and highly portable cameras intended to be worn on the body or attached to objects including vehicles. Most are weather and water resistant and have a wide-angle lens with a field of view greater than 170°. An extensive number of accessories are available which can allow these cameras to be used for obtaining video where it would be otherwise impossible or impractical. Some action cameras allow the user to change the operating characteristics in order to optimise the camera for varying shooting conditions. They are rarely designed to operate in low-light and the battery life may be short. Despite their shortcomings, their small form factor and robust build can be advantageous in some investigation circumstances.

Panoramic view cameras may also provide the investigator with opportunities to obtain video footage that would be otherwise impossible. For example, in order to adequately cover an entire room or space, one would normally require the use of several cameras, each having an overlapping field of view. A single 360° camera placed centrally, can provide a similar level of coverage, with less equipment being necessary. Several varieties of 360° video are available, some only providing the full 360° view in one plane e.g., horizontally, but limiting it in another; other models offer the full 360° in every plane, the resulting video appearing as if taken in the centre of a ball looking outwards. All 360° and other panoramic cameras require additional software in order to view the footage and this will be at a reduced resolution compared to an ordinary video camera. As with action cameras, they often perform poorly in low-light conditions and have a limited battery capacity. Nevertheless, they can provide the investigator with a useful addition to their video taking ability and are worthwhile considering.

16.7.1 *Video thermography*

This refers to video footage taken using a thermal imaging camera. Thermal cameras use thermal radiation in place of light in order to produce an image. Thermal cameras require a special sensor, together with a highly modified lens. The lens, when viewed in ordinary light, has a mirror-like coating to prevent unwanted frequencies of visible and IR light from reaching the sensor. Originally designed for military applications, consumer thermal cameras are primarily designed for the observation and recording of temperature variations. Thermal cameras are also discussed in sections 6 and 7.

The video footage that is obtained using a thermal camera may to all intents and purposes be considered in the same way as that from a conventional video camera. The images are either monochrome or use a false colour representation of the amount of thermal energy and thus the temperature of the scene and objects within it. The image resolution of consumer thermal cameras is very low, even when it is compared to footage from the most basic video camera. Consumer level thermal imaging sensors may only have 80 x 60 or 80 x 120 pixels (0.4 or .09 megapixels). The video refresh rate is also very low, being typically around nine times per second. The resulting video footage is often indistinct and soft and any motion will be blurred. Another problem with the slow frame rate of thermography is that moving objects within the scene can appear ghostly and translucent, which has caused some investigators to consider these normal qualities of thermal video footage as being potentially paranormal.

16.7.2 *Ghost-hunting cameras*

There are an increasing number of video cameras which are advertised and promoted as being specifically intended for use by paranormal investigators. These 'ghost-hunting' video cameras are often consumer models which have been modified in order to meet a perceived need or to exploit a marketing opportunity.

Removing the IR filter is most common, and sometimes the only modification that is carried out. These cameras are then often advertised as being 'full spectrum' cameras, but describing them in this way is misleading. The modification can only increase the amount of IR light that reaches the sensor; it does nothing to improve UV light sensitivity and almost all of the UV light will continue to be absorbed by the lens material and blocked by the optical lens coatings. Another problem for those using one of these ghost-hunting cameras is that of poor quality. The majority of the ghost-hunting cameras offered for sale use an inexpensive, low-quality camera as the basis for the adaption. Many of these donor cameras have a low-resolution sensor, with a fixed focus lens and very poor exposure control. It is common to see a £20 or £30 video camcorder being offered for sale at four or five times the original price, advertised as a specialised ghost investigation tool.

The quality of the various types of modification and adaption that are carried out should also be a concern for users of these cameras. There are few, if any, published specifications for the modification. When inspected, sometimes the only modification was a hefty price increase and the addition of a few decals, the camera appearing to be a perfectly ordinary low-quality model. Without knowing the manner in which the camera has been modified it becomes an almost impossible task to ever determine if an anomaly that is recorded is genuine or merely the result of the modification or adaption. The investigator is advised to avoid using any of these dubiously modified cameras.

Recent developments in ghost detection methods have borrowed video camera systems from the gaming industry. The camera is not used for conventional videography; instead, it is supposed to detect the presence of various spirits and entities. The majority of these systems represent the spirit in the form of a stickman. These devices have become popular with some investigators after their extensive use on several ghost hunting television shows. The manner in which these devices operate is well understood and there is currently nothing to indicate or suggest that they are capable of detecting any paranormal or spiritual entity. Therefore, their use cannot be recommended.

17 | Working with Photographs and Videos

At some point, every investigator is likely to be faced with a photograph or video which contains something that appears to be perplexing or difficult to explain. It is important to understand that simply because it appears to be unusual or an explanation for what has happened cannot be immediately found, it does not automatically mean that it is something that is paranormal or that it is evidence for some paranormal phenomenon. The reality is that although there are a few pictures that remain to be adequately explained, there is still no substantive evidence that anything paranormal has ever been captured using either a camera or video camera.

The advent of photo and video editing software means that it has become common practise for the investigator to load their pictures and footage onto a computer and start adjusting the contrast, brightness and the other settings in an attempt to discern the anomaly. It is unlikely that the individual carrying out the image analysis will be completely unaware of the nature of the investigation and all too often, adjustments are made by someone who already has an idea or belief of what the picture or footage shows; the adjustments they make are either intended to support this notion or are unwittingly influenced by it.

17.1 *Always make a copy*

If the investigator believes that they may have a picture that warrants further attention, it should be protected by removing the memory card in order to prevent any accidental erasure of the picture. If it is not possible to remove the memory card then the picture or video should be marked as being important and copied (do not afterwards delete the original) using the same settings as the original footage or image to an external file store. This can be a connected external memory, computer or cloud storage. Note:

when copying and saving off the device, the investigator should ensure that they select the option to save using the original file size and type as some storage services use compression by default to reduce file size. The copy should be given a meaningful file name. This should contain a reference to the location and the date / time it was taken.

After making a copy, the unchanged original file should be viewed one final time, using the original recording device. This should then be followed by viewing the copy using the device that will be used for examining the image or footage. This step will show any problems which may have occurred during the copying process.

It is recommended that the original pictures and videos or those copies which are being considered in the same way as original recordings, should be retained and archived. The archived images can be used to provide a useful reference source and library which may be useful for when considering other images, either made at the same, or another location.

The following guidance for reviewing and examining a photograph or video recording should be only carried out using a <u>copy</u> of the original recording.

17.2 *Viewing tests*

Once the investigator is satisfied that the copy is an accurate representation of the original then it is recommended that it should be viewed by a number of people. These individuals should be provided with no information about the content of the photograph or video or what they are looking for. Take care to avoid leading statements and questions such as "can you see that figure on the left?" or "look at this picture of a face".

Whenever possible, the viewing tests should be conducted individually. Group viewings carry a greater risk of an individual saying their thoughts out aloud and potentially altering or biasing the opinion of the others.

If the viewer fails to see anything, or asks what they are supposed to be looking at, the investigator should not help or indicate where in a picture, or when in the footage they should pay particular attention. If the viewer sees nothing, then it should be documented accordingly. Viewers should also not be given multiple attempts to watch a video clip or be allowed to spend a lengthy period of time staring at a photograph; the time taken for the viewer to identify the anomaly should be documented.

Immediately after viewing the footage or looking at the picture the viewer should be asked to write down their comments, describing what they can see. This should be done without delay and viewers should not be allowed to change or edit their notes afterwards. When reviewing the comments of the participants, the investigator should consider all of the comments and should not discard any which they themselves disagree with or which are not supportive of either their own opinion or that of the majority of other participants.

17.3 Analysing a picture or video

Many investigators will use a computer with photo or video editing software to view an image and make alterations to it, in order to help them understand what it may show. Often, they will begin by changing the exposure or brightness controls or adjusting some of the other parameters of the image in order to do this. This haphazard method should be avoided. Any changes that are made will usually result in a permanent alteration of the image. Prior to making any changes it is advisable to make and use an additional working copy of the image.

Most of the commercial photo and video editing software that is available is perfectly adequate for many of the steps needed by the investigator to undertake their examination of the image. Unfortunately, the software can add and remove image detail or even substitute entire portions of the original. Due to the ease with which software can be used to subtly change the content of a picture or video, the investigator must take additional steps in order to demonstrate the steps that have been used during the image examination process. The following method is recommended. It will allow every change which has been made to be followed and if necessary, replicated by peer reviewers. Using it will produce a quantity of files and folders and is a more time-consuming process, but it can be used to demonstrate the processes used and to support a conclusion when the investigation results are presented.

- Create a computer folder with a meaningful title that indicates the location and the date / time that the recording took place. Place a first-generation, unaltered copy of the recording into this folder; this will be your reference recording.

- Only ever change one variable or parameter of the sound

at a time and save each change into the computer folder as a new audio file, giving each a meaningful filename or numbering sequence e.g., *locationpicture1.jpg, locationpicture2.jpg* etc.

- It is important that <u>every</u> change that is made is documented. This can easily be done by creating a text file indicating the name and build number of the software that was used and listing every change made to the image using their filenames, e.g. *locationpicture1 – exposure increased by 100%, locationpicture2 – contrast increased by 50%* etc. Save this text file in same folder as the recording.

Occasionally, it may be helpful to apply more radical alterations to the image. These may include changing the saturation, inverting the chroma (colours) or applying a filtering option. The use of any editing tools should always be carefully documented by the investigator, including which were used, the level of the tool that was applied and the order in which they were used.

Ordinarily the software can only assist the investigator; on its own it is incapable of determining what the picture or the video shows. In almost every case, the final decision regarding the content of an image will be a subjective interpretation by the investigator. Their decision should draw together all of the available information relating to the image. This includes the testimony of witnesses, the investigator's knowledge and experience of the location, the prevailing circumstances when the image was taken, and the results from the viewing tests. The investigator should also consider the camera which was used, its placement and the prevailing conditions e.g., lighting etc. It is important that the investigator is aware of the way in which the recording was subsequently handled and examined.

Following analysis or examination, the folder containing the copies and the notes should be retained and archived. This is particularly important with cases that are to be presented for review.

17.3.1 *Use the EXIF metadata*

The Exchangeable Image File Format (EXIF) is an embedded metadata file within every digital photograph. The EXIF data provides information and details about the camera settings and usefully, also the picture. These include the date and time when the picture was taken, the camera's exposure and focus settings, the focal length of the lens and whether the flash was used. In addition, many cameras and particularly, camera-phones add a geo-tag to the EXIF data which gives the precise location where the picture was taken.

Digital photographs do not have an original negative and the EXIF data is the only way that an investigator can demonstrate or check when a picture was taken and the camera settings that were used. For this reason, it is essential that the date and time are correctly set on the camera.

Investigation team members may occasionally forget when a picture was taken or the picture may have been taken by a participant who is not ordinarily a member of the team. Investigators should be aware that some cameras allow the EXIF file to be amended. There are also a number of EXIF editing programs which allow the EXIF data to be overwritten or changed entirely. Sometimes it is possible using additional software to check if the original EXIF data has been overwritten. If the image was taken as part of their own investigation, they must always ascertain why the EXIF metadata is inconsistent or missing. Very rarely it may indicate a software malfunction but it may also indicate fraud or hoax which is not unknown.

Video recordings also have a metadata file embedded within them. It may not be as comprehensive as the EXIF data and apart from the data and time, camera information is usually not available. Some consumer video editing software allows the metadata to be accessed but it may be necessary to use additional software in order to do this. Investigators can also use one of a number of online metadata inspection tools. Video metadata can be used in a similar manner to the EXIF data within photographs and the same cautions should be applied. Geo-tagging information may also be included in most of the popular video formats.

17.4 *The value of photographs and videos*

The investigator should be aware that a photograph or video can easily be altered or have content added to it. Without careful examination of the image and of the supporting metadata it should not be readily accepted as being a true representation of the situation that existed when the image was taken.

Images which are supported by additional information, including data from other objectively gathered measurements and other observations, may have a greater significance and value. For example, in order to develop a case that supports or may contradict the accounts of other experiences and events at the location.

The debate regarding the value of photographs and video recordings made as part of the investigation of a haunting or other related phenomenon continues, but by carefully examining all of the evidence and showing that they have used good practise, the investigator can demonstrate an awareness of the problems and indicate that they have acted to address them.

17.5 *Submitted images*

It is not uncommon for an individual to send a picture or video clip to the investigator for their consideration. Sometimes, they may have discovered something in the image which they are questioning; at other times, it may be sent to support a reported experience or event. Whenever possible, the sender should always be requested to also send the pictures that were taken immediately before, and immediately after, the photograph they are asking the investigator to examine. This will allow the investigator to determine if the photograph is part of a sequence or if it is a unique picture taken in isolation. It also provides the investigator with useful comparative pictures taken using the same camera which may reveal some malfunction of the device.

Typically, the image will be sent to the investigator using email or one of the social media messaging applications. All of these services usually apply data compression which alters the image; often this will be applied without the sender or sometimes the investigator being aware that this has been used. The investigator should request a direct copy of the original image. This may necessitate the sender needing to use a different file transfer method and selecting options that ensure the file is not compressed during the transfer. The investigator may need to advise the sender on how this ought to be done; senders may not be familiar with the steps that are required and these will vary depending on the file transfer service that is used.

The examination of submitted images is the same as that which is used for pictures taken by the investigator and the same process of making and using copies, and documenting every step should be applied. However, a submitted picture should always be given some additional scrutiny and subjected to some additional checks.

17.5.1 *Look at the filename*

Once an image has been received, the first thing the investigator should look at is the file name. Camera manufacturers use a sequential alphanumeric file numbering system; this often indicates the manufacturer, for example, Sony use the DSC prefix followed by a sequence of numbers and Canon use DCF and sequential numbers. If the image that is sent does not conform to this system, for example it is called 'ghostpicture1.jpg', then it is a clear indication that the image has been changed and possibly edited prior to being sent. It is also an indication that the picture has been compressed more than when it was originally taken; every time a jpeg picture is saved, compression algorithms are applied that increasingly compress and reduce the file size.

17.5.2 *Look at the file size*

The size of the file is another good indicator that a change has occurred to the image, either intentionally or during the transfer process. A typical camera-phone that has between 8- and 12-megapixels resolution should be expected to produce an image file of between approximately 3 and 8 megabytes. This is not definitive as it depends upon other variables such as the number of colours in the scene and the levels of compression that the camera applied. Nevertheless, if the file seems inordinately small for the resolution (number of pixels) then it can indicate that the file may have been highly compressed or edited.

17.5.3 *Look at the picture*

The investigator should next consider what the image or the footage is supposed to show. Often, the picture will arrive with a short description saying why it has been sent and what it is supposed to show. Sometimes, the investigator will be presented with an image that the sender claims they took without noticing the anomaly, claiming that it was noticed some time later. The investigator should always try and ascertain why the person decided to take the photograph or video, especially if the content of the picture seems incongruous. People do take unusual images, but pictures of a blank areas of wall or close-up views looking into a window may indicate that the image has been cropped or edited beforehand. Occasionally, the investigator may be sent a picture with the intention of perpetuating a hoax or to bolster a claim that has been made. Such images are increasingly common and done for a variety of reasons. The old adage that 'if something seems too good to be true, then it likely isn't' should apply.

The investigator should not be afraid to ask why such a picture was taken or to seek out additional information about the circumstances and reasons that led to it being taken.

The investigator should explore all of the possibilities and not unquestioningly accept the image and the sender's account, however impressive it may seem.

17.5.4 *Check the metadata*

If the additional pictures requested by the investigator were supplied; the metadata of these should be compared with that of the submitted photograph. This will allow the investigator to quickly ascertain the sequence in which the pictures were taken and the interval between each. It may also reveal any alterations to the sequence of the pictures, the numbering system or the metadata relating the camera settings.

If the metadata or any part of it is missing, particularly anything that relates to the camera's settings, e.g., the shutter speed and focal length of the lens, this is a strong indication that the image has been through one or more additional processes after it was taken. In any submission where a digital photograph has missing or inconsistent metadata, the investigator should request that the person sends an unaltered copy of the original image. If they decline or they claim that the photograph is an unaltered copy of the original; the investigator may decide that they no can longer proceed. However, if they decide to continue, they should be exercise caution and note the metadata was either absent or it contained inconsistencies.

There may be rare occasions when a sender has scanned or digitally copied an analogue photograph that was originally taken using a film camera. In these instances, the metadata will show information pertaining the scanner or camera that was used to make the copy. If the metadata or the sender states that the submitted photograph is a digital reproduction, the investigator is advised to request that they send either the original photograph and if possible, the original film strip or negative.

Sometimes, the metadata may reveal other helpful information, e.g., if the submitted photograph has been copied from another source including the internet or social media. The metadata should also be compared with the sender's description of the experience or the events. Not everyone will assiduously set the date and time on their camera but if the metadata contains a geo-tag indicating it was taken somewhere other than where the sender claims it was taken, or if it shows that the flash was used and the person says that it was not; the investigator must clarify these discrepancies with the sender.

17.5.5 *Look at the negative*

In the case of analogue photographs that are submitted, the investigator may occasionally be able to obtain the corresponding film strip or negative. This is the original medium onto which the image was taken. This may often reveal additional information that will not be contained in the print or a digital copy.

After all of the available pictures have been taken, the film then needs to be developed using a temperature and light sensitive, multi-stage chemical process. This process can produce many of the apparent anomalies that are presented for examination. The developing process may be incomplete, leading to areas of differential developing. Water marks caused by poor drying after developing are common; many of these water blemishes are surprisingly human-like in their appearance.

The negative can also reveal problems or faults with the camera; poor light seals around the film compartment can cause streaks and oddly coloured regions in the final picture. Poor handling of the film is also common and may be seen as darker regions at the top or bottom edges of the film strip. People, often used to leave a partially exposed film in their camera for lengthy periods and this would cause the film to deteriorate, the light sensitive layers gradually losing their sensitivity and causing irregular patches of colour to appear.

Occasionally, the negative can reveal problems which occurred during the printing of the photograph. This too, is a multi-stage, light and temperature sensitive process, with several opportunities to introduce anomalies. These, will however only manifest in the print and are not present on the negative. Many of the anomalies caused by the printing stage may appear similar to those which can happen in the developing stage, but their absence on the negative lets the investigator make an accurate assessment of when the anomaly was introduced into the photograph.

18 | Smartphones and Tablet Computers

Investigators have not been slow to adopt smartphones and tablet computer technology to support their investigations. A great deal of the early use has involved the investigator using one or more of the numerous 'ghost hunting' applications (Apps). Ghost detecting radars and spirit communication Apps abound in the various App stores. Other popular Apps emulate established and popular ghost hunting tools including the Ouija board, EMF meters and EVP devices. In reality, many of these programs are merely software trickery. Some of the Apps do make use of the device's built-in array of sensors, but this is often done in a way that provides the user with no usable data or information about how the sensors are being used.

Disregarding the ghost hunting Apps, a smartphone or tablet can be used to provide the investigator with a great deal of high-quality data, relating to a number of physical variables. Developments in smartphone and tablet technology over the past decade means that these devices are now a significant additional resource for investigators.

The camera built into many smartphones can often match or surpass the quality and performance of a consumer level digital camera or video camera. Its use should be considered in exactly the same way as any other still or video camera (see **Secs. 15 & 16**). Smartphone cameras do use a small format image sensor and most will have either a fixed or limited range of available apertures. The lens is normally a fixed focal length and zooming is done digitally. Several models may have more than one camera, allowing the investigator to choose different viewpoints, sometimes simultaneously.

The major downside for those wishing to use a smartphone camera for their investigations is the high degree of automation that is normally used by these built-in camera systems. Software is used to control almost every aspect of the picture or video taking process and the user interface may only offer a limited range of options for changing the camera's settings or for controlling the exposure and focus. Where options to change settings are provided, they are often accessible only by using a series of menus which may be time consuming and frustrating. The standard camera software may also be limited to only basic operating controls and may require additional Apps to be installed in order to access all of the camera's functionality or to disable some of the less helpful automation.

The audio recorder on most smartphones and tablets is capable of recording high quality sound. Unfortunately, the sound recording software that is supplied with the device is often intended only for basic audio note taking, with limited options to change the audio settings. There are several Apps available which do allow the user to make recordings which will exceed the sound quality from many of the portable recorders that are popular with investigators. The built-in microphone is primarily intended to accurately reproduce the human voice and the very small capsule requires high levels of signal amplification, especially when used for recording quiet sounds. It is recommended that the investigator obtains an external microphone (**see Sec. 12**) to ensure the best quality audio recording possible from their device. Depending upon the device, the method for connecting an external microphone will vary and users are advised to check the external microphone is compatible with the device they are using.

In addition to the camera and sound recorder, many smartphones and tablet computers have a suite of highly accurate sensors that are built in to the device. These can include a magnetometer, accelerometer, light intensity sensor and a barometer. Some of the recent models incorporate additional sensors, e.g., a LIDAR (LIght Distance and Ranging) sensor, which is able to make very accurate distance measurements and can render a three-dimensional representation of a location and the objects inside to a high degree of accuracy.

Several of the built-in sensors can be used on their own, or in combination, to make measurements of the physical environment within and around a location. They can also be used to make other measurements and observations which are of potential value to an investigator. For example, the accelerometer can measure vibration and acceleration forces which can be helpful when studying the motion of objects and the forces acting upon them. The magnetometer can measure an object's tilt and rotation, which is often reported in table-tilting experiments. Connecting a measuring microphone allows the sound recorder to be used as a high-quality sound level meter, capable of carrying out complex frequency measurements.

In addition to the built-in sensors, smartphones and tablets can be connected to an array of external sensors, allowing the investigator to make an even greater or more accurate range of measurements and observations. External sensors include; seismometers, thermometers of different types, thermal imaging cameras, strain gauges, motion sensors and radiation detectors for both non-ionising and ionising radiation. Linking the device to a smartwatch or other body worn sensors makes it possible to observe and measure a range of biometric parameters including heart-rate, electrocardiogram (ECG), blood oxygen level and body temperature. Hardware and software options are available, which cover almost every physical and environmental variable the investigator may wish to measure. The availability of options depends upon the device and its operating system. For investigators considering using a smartphone or tablet in this way, it is recommended that they undertake an internet search using the variable which is to be measured and the make and model of the particular device, e.g., 'temperature and iPhone 8' as the search terms for additional information about the Apps and any additional items that may be required.

18.1 *Problems using smart devices*

Smartphones and tablet computers have their own unique set of problems and considerations, that must be properly addressed by investigators. The technology, particularly relating to its use in gathering personal biometric data, is intrusive and ethical issues must be carefully considered and addressed before it is used.

Accessories can interfere with the proper operation of some sensors; for instance, the magnetic closure that is used in some protective cases can adversely affect the accuracy and operation of the built-in magnetometer, and a shock absorbing case may protect the device, but it will significantly reduce the sensitivity of the accelerometer when the device is being used to measure vibration.

The connectivity of the device, either via the mobile phone network, Wi-Fi or Bluetooth, can adversely affect the operation of several of the sensors. Using airplane mode may partially disable some of these services but it doesn't always provide a complete solution to interference that is caused by the systems and services which are running within the device itself. Other problems can usually be fixed by changing the settings on the device or within the settings provided by the software App. This may require the user to work through a series of menus and numerous options. The importance of becoming familiar with the operation of a device before any investigation use has been mentioned elsewhere in these notes. It relates as much to using smartphones and tablets as it does to every other item of equipment that the investigator may use.

Although the device may contain a number of sensors, the operating system may restrict the number of applications which can be used simultaneously. Investigators may therefore need to prioritise the measurements or functions they wish to use and set up the device in different ways to accommodate each of these functions in turn.

Some smartphones and tablets have a fixed amount of memory that cannot be increased and investigators may have to consider the number of pictures or the duration of video footage. Some devices do allow additional memory to be plugged in or cloud storage options to be used, but users should ensure that the selected options for these services are set so as to retain the original image and recording quality as some cloud storage services have default options which prioritise the speed of the data transfer and reduce the image quality in order to achieve this.

Battery life may be restrictive; some of the external sensors may also draw their power from the device itself, further limiting the available battery. Many smartphones and tablets are able to use an external power source but this often uses the same connection method as a desired external sensor and an adaptor which allows several simultaneous connections, including power, may be required. Turning off unwanted Apps and limiting the device's connectivity can also increase the battery life. The use of streaming services may need to be limited and the uploading of data or stored recordings and images can be carried out during convenient breaks in the investigation.

The use of any of the sensors or systems on the device, for example, the camera, audio recorder, magnetometer or an external thermometer, should be considered in the same way as for a stand-alone instrument which is used for the same purposes.

Smartphones and tablets are undoubtedly set to become more powerful and even more capable in the future and it is worthwhile considering using this type of device either alongside, or as a direct replacement for, other items of equipment that may already be in use or which the investigator may be considering using in the future.

However, the technology isn't the major consideration with

these smart devices. They are capable of holding a huge amount of personal and sensitive information. Whenever any of these smart devices are being used, even if it is only by members of the investigation team or others who are directly involved in the case; it is important that any data that is obtained is handled with great care and sensitivity (**see Sec. 3.1**).

19 | Spontaneous Object Movement

The reported spontaneous movement of objects in cases of haunting is commonplace and is even more likely to be reported in cases of apparent poltergeist manifestation. The objects themselves may vary considerably in both size and weight and the nature of their movement also varies considerably from case to case.

Investigators have sought to objectively study and document these occurrences using a variety of techniques. One of the most common methods is the use of a video camera in order to try and capture and record any movements for later examination. Another popular method is to use some form of motion sensing device. These range from basic devices which have an audible or visual alarm to more advanced systems which are able to activate additional recording or measuring apparatus.

It is not always necessary to apply technology in order to demonstrate that an object has moved. Earlier generations of investigators used the simple and very effective technique of drawing a chalk or pencil line around any object which they suspected of moving or being moved. This allowed them to quickly see if any displacement had occurred and by using a tape measure, they could determine the amount of movement which had taken place. Another simple method, that is useful with larger objects such as doors, is to tape a sheet of paper onto the floor and to also tape a pencil to the door so that it just touches the paper. Any movement of the door will then be indicated by a pencil line on the paper and the extent of the motion determined by measuring the length of the line.

Investigators who opt for using a video camera to capture movement must ensure that adequate consideration has been given to all of the potential causes for any motion that is observed. Often, the investigator will direct the camera's viewpoint upon the object of interest, failing to show very much, if anything at all, of the surrounding scene. This not only increases the likelihood of them missing a possible cause which lies outside of the camera's field of view, but will inevitably lead others to question the validity of their evidence. The investigator is advised to consider using a wider field of view or to use two video cameras; one with a narrow field of view centred upon the object, and the second camera taking a wider viewpoint. If resources allow, additional cameras may sometimes be helpful; providing additional views from the side, rear or above the object. The aim is to demonstrate that the investigator has considered all of the potential causes of any movement and that each possibility has been covered to the best of the investigator's capability.

It is often helpful to consider the event from the perspective of someone who is deeply sceptical; what explanations might they offer if presented with footage of the object moving? Use that as a starting point when designing your experiment. Consider the lighting conditions and the camera's viewpoint; are there any areas which are obscured from the camera's view, in which a person or some device for introducing movement might be concealed? What about nearby people? Can they be clearly seen and be shown not to have interfered with the object, either wittingly or unwittingly?

Occasionally, spontaneous movements which are recorded by video may be so subtle that they may be missed when reviewing the footage afterwards. If movement is suspected, it is often helpful to play back the recording at two or three times the normal speed; this technique can sometimes reveal slow or subtle movements to the investigator.

Video surveillance may not always be possible or practical. In these circumstances the use of a motion sensing device may be beneficial. Properly positioned, a motion detector can be used to indicate the presence of a person or an animal who may otherwise have gone unnoticed. Motion detectors, often sold as burglar alarms, are readily available and inexpensive. Most operate by detecting an increase in the amount of infra-red thermal energy caused by the body heat of a person or animal. Devices that operate in a similar manner to car reversing sensors are also available; these emit an inaudible, ultra-high frequency sound and detect any change to the sound that is reflected back from the surroundings. This type of detector has the advantage of being able to detect movement by objects that are at the same ambient temperature as their surroundings. Beam-barrier devices are another common means of detecting motion and operate by emitting an invisible infra-red beam which is detected, either by a separate receiver device or by means of a reflector that returns the light to the emitter / receiver. If the light path is interrupted or broken by a person or an object then the alarm is sounded.

In some circumstances, the investigator may wish to carry out a more detailed examination of any detected or observed motion. This can be achieved by using an accelerometer, which is an electronic component capable of measuring extremely small amounts of motion. Until recently, accelerometers were costly and needed to be permanently connected to a computer in order to function, but affordable USB data logging accelerometers are now available which can precisely measure and record movement or vibration in any direction for extended periods. Many smartphones and tablet devices include a three-axis accelerometer; this can be used to measure the motion of any object the device is placed upon. In order to work effectively, the smartphone must be securely attached to the object and therefore this technique may only be suitable for use with larger objects such as tables.

19.1 *Trigger objects*

A popular method with investigators is the use of a trigger object. These are items which are placed around the investigation site and are intended to provoke some sort of response by the ghost or spirit, either by moving or interfering with the object.

A common technique for carrying out a trigger object experiment is to place the object onto a sheet of paper, drawing around it in order to mark its position. This is similar to the method used by early investigators including Harry Price and Peter Underwood. Price referred to the items which he placed into various locations as 'control objects', marking their position by circling the items with chalk or pencil; Underwood, used the same method, describing the items he placed as 'evocative articles'.

If the investigator opts to use this method, they must be able to demonstrate that all normal means of movement can be excluded. This is more difficult when items are left unattended for extended periods, which is a common practise for those who use trigger objects. Continuous video recording is the most obvious means of showing that the unattended object was not interfered with, but, as with other instances of spontaneous movement, the investigator should carefully consider the placement and viewpoint of the camera. Sometimes, the trigger object is placed directly onto a surface, sometimes with little regard being given to the type of the surface that it is placed upon. The surface may slope or it may be wet or slippery. In some circumstances, the surface itself may be subject to vibration and movement which can cause the trigger object to move. If the trigger object is placed onto a sheet of paper, the investigator must ensure that the paper cannot easily be moved by draughts of air or by being intentionally blown upon by someone. Taping the paper to the surface in order to prevent it from moving is a simple remedy in this situation.

Trigger objects which contain some type of electronic indicator are available and have become popular with investigators. Amongst the most popular of these, are small transparent balls containing motion activated flashing lights. These were originally intended as toys for pet cats and their spherical shape requires very little force in order to make them to move. They are inherently unstable due to the batteries and lights being unevenly distributed inside the ball, resulting in any motion appearing erratic or unusual. They are also sensitive to vibration and in some instances, this can cause the lights to flash with no apparent cause.

In recent years, an assortment of children's toys has been used by investigators, particularly in locations where the spirits of children are reputed to manifest. The toys are often perfectly ordinary soft toys which have been retrofitted with one or more electronic sensors. A variety of sensors are available; some react to changes in temperature, others to changes within the surrounding electro-magnetic field and some have a simple motion sensing alarm. Regardless of the particular toy or the type of sensor that has been fitted, none of these objects can ever provide the investigator with any worthwhile information. The sensors are rudimentary and have uncertain activation thresholds which cannot be adjusted. Often, the investigator is presented with just a set of coloured lights and sounds that give no worthwhile information about any variable which the toy is claimed to be measuring. Many of these trigger object toys are also expensive and they are often promoted with dubious and unsupported claims regarding their usefulness. The investigator is advised to consider these points very carefully before purchasing and using any of these electronic ghost hunting toys.

19.2 *Understanding spontaneous object movement*

Occasionally, the investigator will discover that their video footage shows an object that is moving without apparent cause or in an unusual manner. It is then necessary for them to try to determine the cause of the observed motion. The video footage can be useful in these circumstances, not only as evidence of and for the object's movement, but as a means for discovering more about that motion. For example, it is possible to determine the precise speed at which the object is moving using the frame rate of the video footage. This is the number of individual frames which are taken each second, e.g., 30 frames per second (fps), 60 fps etc. The timecode for each of these frames offers a highly accurate time indicator which can be accessed with ordinary video editing software.

The video can also be viewed frame by frame, giving the investigator an opportunity to watch the entire sequence in a step-wise manner that may sometimes reveal additional information that might have gone unnoticed when watching the ordinary playback. Depending upon the object and the type of motion that has been observed it may be possible to use the data from other items of equipment in order to examine possible causes. For example, a thermal imager may reveal a source of thermal air currents; measuring vibrations may disclose a mechanical cause such as machinery or passing heavy traffic. For larger objects, attaching an accelerometer to it will provide data about the way in which it moved and the forces that were applied to make it start or to make it stop.

Any observed motion for which the cause cannot be determined should not automatically lead to a presumption that the motion must have a paranormal cause. It only demonstrates that the cause has not yet been found. In these instances, the equipment may be assistive. Data from other sensors should be examined, including sound recordings and other measurements that were made at and around the time that the object movement took place. For example, accelerometer data might indicate that the investigation site is subjected to periodic vibrations or camera footage may show passing traffic or human and animal activity occurring just before or whilst the object moves. Often, the extra data may be inconclusive, but occasionally it may be sufficient for the investigator to consider further possible causes and they may decide to undertake additional measurements and tests in order to test their predictions.

19.3 *Shades and apparitions*

From time to time the investigator may discover movement in their video footage that is not immediately attributable to an object or person. Sometimes, this movement will take the form of indistinct shadows and shapes; occasionally, it may resemble a figure, either entire or in part. The investigator is cautioned against making any presumption that this represents the appearance of an apparition or anything else that is untoward. The investigator should closely examine the video footage for additional clues; the video may show people moving about or the illumination from screens and the lights on items of their equipment. Occasionally, the observed motion may not be real, but is the result of movement by the camera's focussing mechanism or it may be the result of compression artifacts in the video footage. Oftentimes, the cause may never be properly determined, but it is sometimes worthwhile also examining the data from other items of equipment. For example, there may be an audio recording of a passing vehicle that coincides with the observed motion in the video footage. The data may ultimately be inconclusive, but it may occasionally suggest a possible cause which the investigator can test by carrying out additional tests and measurements.

20 | Measuring Other Things

Investigators have always cast their net widely in the search for evidence of ghosts, apparitions, poltergeists and similar phenomena. This has resulted in them considering the observation and measurement of a range of environmental variables in addition to those which are more commonly considered.

20.1 *Carbon monoxide*

Some investigators claim that high levels of carbon monoxide (CO) have been found during investigations of many haunted locations. This claim is hard to test but some of the symptoms of CO exposure are similar to those which are associated with claims of paranormal experiences, e.g., visual disturbance, personality change and unusual emotional behaviour. Carbon monoxide is a colourless, odourless gas which is produced by fuel burning appliances, e.g., heaters, stoves, internal combustion engines etc. The level of CO is measured in parts per million (ppm) i.e., the number of CO molecules per million molecules of air. In an average home, CO levels of between 0.5 and 10ppm are considered normal. However, prolonged exposure to levels of 20 to 30ppm can cause symptoms to occur and at levels exceeding 100ppm individuals are at significant risk and should evacuate the area.

Carbon monoxide detectors and measuring devices are already fitted in many locations. These range from simple patch indicators that change colour if exposed to CO for an extended period to monitoring systems which provide a real-time measurement of the CO levels that are present.

Carbon monoxide patch indicators are an unreliable method for determining the presence of the gas and provide no worthwhile data. The most commonly used devices are CO alarms, which operate an alarm when the levels of CO become excessive or prolonged. The level at which the alarm activates is fixed and not user adjustable. Using a simple CO alarm is unlikely to provide the investigator with sufficient data to be helpful. However, they are advised to heed any alarm activation and remove themselves and anyone else from the location.

If the investigator intends to measure the levels of CO that are present then their only realistic option is to use a device that indicates the level in real-time. Inexpensive devices are available that have a numerical readout in ppm. These can be periodically checked and the data recorded manually. Data-logging CO monitors are also available which can record the levels over time. As with any measuring device, the manufacturer's instructions should be followed. Detectors should be placed at least one metre from any fuel burning appliance and at the normal head height (breathing level) of the occupants.

20.2 *Ionising radiation*

Geiger counters are increasingly being used by some investigators, despite there being little, if anything at all, to suggest that measuring ionising radiation at haunted locations is worthwhile. Most likely, this is a result of investigators confusing ionising nuclear radiation with non-ionising electromagnetic radiation. There are several types of ionising radiation: Alpha and beta particles are charged protons, neutrons and electrons that are emitted by the radioactive decay of atoms; these do not form part of the electromagnetic spectrum. Gamma and x-rays are high energy electromagnetic emissions in the form of photons; they are also produced by radioactive decay (gamma rays) or they may be artificially produced (x-rays). Cosmic radiation hitting the Earth from space is also considered as being gamma radiation. Ionising radiation is present at every location, produced by the minerals in the surrounding ground and cosmic rays. Some construction materials may also emit small amounts of alpha, beta and gamma radiation.

The most common method of measuring the levels of ionising radiation is by means of a Geiger counter; other devices are also used, for example, a scintillometer; these are expensive and unlikely to be used by paranormal investigators. Geiger counters are constructed of a thin-walled glass tube, sometimes incorporating a mica window at one end in order to allow alpha particles to be detected. Tubes constructed entirely of glass are only capable of detecting beta, gamma and x-ray emissions. The rate of detection by the Geiger tube depends upon the size and construction of the detector; thus, the same emission source may give different readings on devices using different detection tubes. Geiger tubes are generally unable to distinguish between a beta particle or a gamma wave emission and some tubes will also respond to alpha particles.

Ionising radiation levels decrease as the distance from the source is increased and conforms to the inverse square law. For example, if the distance from the source doubles the level of radiation decreases to one quarter and if the distance increases by a factor of ten the level is reduced by a factor of one hundred.

Radiation levels can be expressed in a number of ways; this may be related to human exposure levels using units of Sieverts per hour (SI unit) or Rem per hour, or simply the number of radioactive disintegrations per second using units of Becquerel (SI Unit) and Curie. Some devices indicate the amount of radioactivity using the number of times that the tube detects a single radioactive emission; this is expressed using counts per minute (cpm) or counts per second (cps). This method is the most helpful means of making comparative measurements of radioactivity.

It is questionable if measuring radioactivity at a location is of any value to the investigator. Exposure to ionising radiation is asymptomatic unless the received dose is extremely high. Low levels of radiation typically require very long periods of exposure, i.e., years, before any signs or symptoms become apparent. Despite their continued popularity with investigators, the use of Geiger counters cannot be recommended.

20.3 *Radon gas*

Radon is a naturally occurring odourless radioactive gas that is produced by radioactive decay. In sufficient quantities, long term exposure to Radon can be injurious to health and is an established cause of lung cancer. Depending upon the underlying geology, parts of the country are more likely to have higher ambient levels of Radon than others, and in areas where Radon levels are high then precautions to reduce the levels are used. Radon exposure ordinarily takes years to manifest as a health problem and those who are exposed are asymptomatic until the disease is at an advanced stage. There is nothing to suggest that Radon exposure is a factor in any reported paranormal experience and there is no reason for investigators to be measuring Radon levels at any location site.

20.4 *Air ions*

Air ions are electrically charged air molecules or atoms. If the molecule has ejected an electron, it has an overall positive charge whilst those which attract or gain an electron have a negative charge. Negatively charged air molecules are used in industrial and domestic dust removal systems and are commonly used in devices which claim health and wellbeing benefits from their use. Positive and negative air ions can be produced naturally or they may be man-made. Positive air ions are produced by volcanos, burning materials, high voltage discharge from radio transmitters and released by some chemicals. Negative ions are produced by sunlight, atmospheric electrical discharges and whenever water collides with itself, e.g., in ocean waves and waterfalls. They can also be produced by ionisers intended for industrial or domestic use. There are some studies which have suggested that negatively charged air ions may have a role in promoting wellbeing or that positive air ions may be linked to poor health. The data is not conclusive but there are many who contend that in addition to their use in air purification systems, air ions are also significant to our general health and welfare.

A number of investigators routinely measure the amount of charged air particles (ions) that are present at the investigation site. This seems rooted in ideas and suggestions that the charged air particles can in some ways supply energy to the manifesting ghost or spirit. This has also led to some investigators using domestic ionisers in an attempt to generate excess quantities of energy in the form of negative ions into some locations, hoping that this will increase the overall levels of paranormal activity.

A significant problem with measuring the level of air ions is that the detectors are inherently inaccurate. Some of the more popular devices that are used by investigators have a measuring accuracy of less than 25%. Many of the devices provide no means of indicating the level of ions but simply indicate when an (often) unspecified level has been reached.

The overall lack of accuracy means that these devices offer no significant value to the investigator or to their understanding of the conditions which prevail at the location. Their use cannot be commended and the investigator should waste little time attempting to measure or produce air ions.

20.5 *Static electricity*

As the name implies, static electricity refers to any electrical charge that is unable to discharge itself or move, thereby producing an electrical current. The static electrical charge can be positive or negative. A static electrical charge does not move and therefore has no associated magnetic field and cannot be detected by using an EMF meter, even one that has an electric field mode. Static electrical charges can be produced by rubbing together two insulating materials (triboelectric effect), by the heating of some materials (pyroelectric effect), by applying mechanical stress to a material (piezoelectric effect) and by the proximity of a charged material with a neutrally charged material (electrostatic induction).

Opposite static charges attract one another whilst two charges having the same polarity will oppose one another. This is similar to the effect which can be observed with magnets and the opposing or attracting electrical forces can be sometimes be strong enough to cause small objects to move. This has been suggested as the cause of some observed instances of spontaneous movement in séance rooms or haunted locations. Exposure to static electricity can create some unusual physical effects, predominantly sensations of being lightly touched or stroked, the result of body hair moving as it becomes charged. More noticeable physical effects are head and body hair sticking up and the occasional sparks or minor shocks when the static electricity is discharged. Static electrical charges are unable to penetrate the skin and there are no indications that exposure causes any adverse physiological effects. Apart from the limited physical manifestations, there is little to suggest that any connection exists between reported paranormal events and experiences and exposure to static electrical charges.

Detecting the presence of static electrical charges can easily be done using an electroscope, which is a simple device made from two thin sheets of metal or conductive plastic. The applied electrical charge causes the two sheets to move apart and the amount of movement can be used to roughly indicate the amount of charge. The electroscope is unable to determine the polarity of the charge or accurately quantify the amount of charge. Accurately measuring the static electrical charge requires either an electrostatic field meter which displays the amount of charge in units of volts per metre (V/m) or a static locator meter which displays the charge in Volts. Both of these are highly expensive options and both have very limited operating parameters in which they will work.

Due to the cost limitations and the difficulty involved in making accurate measurements, and the lack of any indication of a connection between reported experiences and static electricity, there is little reason to suggest that investigators should overly concern themselves with measuring this particular variable. For investigators who do wish to ascertain the presence of a static electrical charge they will almost certainly be better served by making or buying a simple electroscope.

20.6 *Vibration*

There are a number of devices that are used by investigators in order to observe or measure vibrations. Early investigators used a bowl containing Mercury or water to observe vibrations which may be present. Vibrations caused by the passage of underground water or seismic activity has been suggested as the cause of motions that have been observed in some instances of hauntings and poltergeist cases, but limited testing has shown this to be unlikely. Vibrations may also indicate the presence of infrasound, which has been shown to increase the likelihood of some individuals reporting paranormal experiences.

Vibration can be measured in a number of ways; for example, by referring to its frequency or the number of oscillations per second, expressed in Hertz (Hz): the velocity of the motion, expressed in millimetres per second (mm/s): the acceleration, or the rate at which the velocity is changing, measured in metres per second squared (m/s2) or in units of gravitational constant 'g' (1g = 9.81m/s2).

Vibration meters or stand-alone vibration sensors, are able to precisely measure the vibration, but they are often an expensive option. The investigator may instead use the accelerometer that is built-into their smartphone or tablet computer. This method provides accurate and precise data for motion in any axis. There are some technical limitations to the sensor but these will not affect the majority of the measurements that are carried out for the purposes of investigating. Plug-in and Bluetooth connected vibration sensors can be used to increase the accuracy and precision of the measurements.

Understanding vibration can be a complex subject and investigators may find themselves deterred when trying to understand the data that is produced. This problem is often compounded by the way in which the data is presented using the small screen of the device. Many of the Apps for measuring vibration or acceleration forces have help files and frequently asked questions (FAQ's) that can be used to assist the investigator. Oftentimes, the investigator may only require some of the information; for example, the frequency of the vibration. Options to turn off unwanted measuring axes or to select maximum and minimum levels or peak hold functions can be helpful.

There are several devices which indicate vibration in a crude manner, sometimes with only a light or buzzer. Setting the alert threshold for these is also a crude affair with a basic unmarked rotary control being provided. These devices are frequently used by investigators as a means of communicating with the supposed spirit or ghost. The entity is invited to communicate by activating the device's alarm and to use these activations as a means of answering questions that are asked aloud by the investigator. Notwithstanding the crude nature and operation of the device itself, any evidence that is claimed by misusing the device in this way will be open to serious doubt and will do little, if anything, to enhance the credibility of the investigation.

20.7 *Light*

Light can be measured in a number of ways, for example the amount of light that falls onto a given area which is measured in lux or the intensity of the light source, measured in lumens. The lumen value will normally be fixed, determined by the type of light source that is being used; the lux value will increase or decrease as the distance from the light source is altered. Lux values change in accordance with the inverse square law. The colour of the light can also be measured in terms of its colour temperature, in degrees Kelvin (°K).

Light meters are often used by investigators. These devices are primarily used by photographers to set the exposure controls of their camera and the majority of light meters can be used to either measure lux or lumen. A number of smartphones are able to accurately measure both lux and lumen, and depending on the particular App that is used they can also be used to measure the colour temperature. The sensor in light meters (and smartphones) has a specific field of view which widens as the distance from the sensor is increased. If the region that is being measured is not accurately aligned with the sensor's field of view the accuracy of the measurements will be adversely affected.

The rationale for using a lux meter on an investigation is unclear; a popular use is for the detection of supposed shadow people or entities. As the name suggests, these black forms are without detail and are commonly reported by witnesses and investigators. The investigator observes the lux meter for unexpected dips in the light level as a means for detecting these dark entities. Other investigators use the lux meter as a method for communicating with the ghost or spirit, inviting it to interfere with the device to indicate their presence or to answer questions put by the investigator.

There are very few occasions where an investigator may need to accurately measure the light, either the intensity of the source or the ambient levels at a location. Using a light meter seems to be a case of measure anything and everything, hoping to discover something that is anomalous.

20.8 *Dowsing rods and pendulums*

Some form of dowsing rod or pendulum is found in the equipment used by many investigators. Often, these will be home-made or sometimes they may be one of several types that are advertised for investigation use. Dowsing is usually associated with searching for water and mineral deposits and there are some anecdotal indications that it may sometimes be successful in these situations. Dowsing in order to locate ghosts or spirits, or to determine the presence of some unspecified form of energy, which is conducive to their manifesting, has nothing to suggest that it is worthwhile. The investigator has no means of verifying the results of their endeavours and any results are of questionable value to the overall investigation.

20.9 *Torches (flashlights)*

The torch (flashlight) is arguably the most common item to be found amongst the equipment used by investigators. Used to provide illumination, torches are available in a range of lighting colours and brightness levels. Human night vision can take between twenty minutes to an hour (or longer) to reach its full potential and night adaption can be significantly impaired by even a short exposure to bright light. A dim red light may be helpful at night as it can minimise any excessive glare or dazzle which would diminish the ability of the eyes to adapt to low light conditions. A drawback to using red light is that the human eye is least sensitive to this colour and visual acuity will be decreased and this may cause individuals to misperceive what they are seeing and subsequently reporting.

Some investigators have begun to use lighting of other colours, blue and green are increasingly popular. Neither are as effective for protecting the night adaption of the eyes but if sufficiently dim they may be useful for some individuals or in some locations. There is rarely any occasion when a powerful torch with an output of hundreds of lumens will be required during an investigation; using such a torch significantly increases the potential for the investigator either dazzling themselves or the other members of the investigation party.

20.9.1 *Communicating using a torch*

Aside from the torch providing useful illumination, some investigators have started to experiment using the torch as a device for communicating with spirits or ghosts. There seems to be no clear rationale for this idea gaining prominence and it is presently restricted to only being effective with a particular make and model of torch e.g., the AA size mini-Maglite ®. This model has an aluminium alloy body and is operated by means of a screw-cap switch. The investigator asks aloud a series of questions to which the entity apparently responds by turning the torch on and off. In order for this method to work successfully the investigator is required to turn the tail-cap switch of the torch so that the bulb is just lit. The torch can then be placed down somewhere convenient and the questions commenced. It is well understood that the subsequent turning on and off of the torch is not due to any paranormal force or the intervention of any spirit or other entity and except for the purposes of an amusing party trick, investigators have no reasons to be using this method as part of any investigation.

21 | Additional Resources

With such a vast array of equipment now being used by investigators, it is beyond the scope of these guidance notes to answer every question that arises, or to suggest methods for using the equipment in every type of case. Fortunately, the investigator has unrivalled access to a vast wealth of additional information which they can draw upon.

The first port of call should always be the instruction manual and specifications that are supplied by the manufacturer; these may be printed and supplied with the device or they may be available to download from the manufacturer's website. This can be done before ever purchasing or acquiring a device and is helpful when considering the purchase of a new item of equipment. Often, the online manual and specification data will contain much more information than the supplied printed material, which is often just a quick-start guide and a list of the main functions.

There are also thousands of pages of information that are freely available, in online technical libraries and journals, specialist media publications and academic resources. Bookstores and libraries are another rich resource for books that deal with many of the things that an investigator will be interested in measuring. Investigators should not limit the scope of their research or the resources that they draw from; many hobby magazines contain useful how-to guides and tips for using items of equipment, and even school textbooks are a great place to find information about the physical processes which the investigator often needs to measure and observe.

Unfortunately, it is necessary to warn investigators about the way in which some pieces of equipment are portrayed and used in many paranormal television shows. The aim of these shows is primarily to entertain their audience and little thought or attention is ever given to how any equipment is described or used. A similar level of caution should also be used when reading or viewing social media pages which are often used to promote personal belief and untestable ideas. It is always good to acquaint oneself with current practise and the results of others who may be using similar items of equipment, but this can also reveal poor methods and misleading claims.

Those who still have questions may consider directing them to one of the learned and well-established organisations that exist for the study of spontaneous cases. This includes the Society for Psychical Research, The Association for the Scientific Study of Anomalous Phenomena (ASSAP) and The Ghost Club. Some universities have departments that maintain an interest in spontaneous cases who may be able to answer your question or direct your enquiry to an appropriate person or department.

22 | In Conclusion

The use of equipment has become a mainstay of every investigation of poltergeists and hauntings. In many instances the equipment can provide the investigator with helpful data and worthwhile information. Unfortunately, it can also provide the investigator with unhelpful data and misleading information. This is rarely the fault of the equipment; most of the problems are caused by the investigator misusing the equipment, misunderstanding the data it is providing or failing to use that data to its best potential.

Undoubtedly, the capabilities of the equipment will continue to improve and it will become more accurate and more precise and new ways to examine our surroundings will emerge.

Equipment will also become more affordable and more accessible to a greater number of investigators. As an example, in 2006, a basic thermal imaging camera cost several thousands of pounds and was able to store a few thermographs and display a single temperature point. Just fifteen years later, a thermal imager can be bought for just a few hundreds of pounds; it provides greater accuracy, allows thermographic video to be taken and has the capability to display the temperature in dozens of user selected points.

The improving technology offers many benefits but it also comes with drawbacks that will undoubtedly challenge investigators. Photography has benefitted immensely from advancements in sensor technology and ever more powerful image writing software. Photographs and videos may now be taken under almost any lighting conditions with comparative ease; but the value of photographs and video recordings has been much diminished by the ease with which false ghosts can be created.

It is unlikely that there will ever be a device or piece of equipment that can demonstrate the reality of ghosts, apparitions or poltergeists; but diligent investigations may reveal much about why people report these phenomena and teach us a great deal about these fascinating human experiences. The real advancements in our knowledge won't come from the equipment, but from how that equipment is used and how the information that it provides is used. The investigator will continue to be the most important part of the investigation process.

Lightning Source UK Ltd.
Milton Keynes UK
UKHW021843060721
386731UK00004B/103